EXPEDITIONS TO SUCCESS

Journeying with God in the Workplace

EXPEDITIONS TO SUCCESS

Journeying with God in the Workplace

JOE SCHURINGA

LifeWork Project

Published by
Hasmark Publishing International
www.hasmarkpublishing.com

Copyright © 2020 Johan Frederik Schuringa

First Edition

No part of this book may be reproduced or transmitted in any form or by any means, electronic or mechanical, including photocopying, recording or by any information storage and retrieval system, without written permission from the author, except for the inclusion of brief quotations in a review.

Disclaimer

This book is designed to provide information and motivation to our readers. It is sold with the understanding that the publisher is not engaged to render any type of psychological, legal, or any other kind of professional advice. The content of each article is the sole expression and opinion of its author, and not necessarily that of the publisher. No warranties or guarantees are expressed or implied by the publisher's choice to include any of the content in this volume. Neither the publisher nor the individual author(s) shall be liable for any physical, psychological, emotional, financial, or commercial damages, including, but not limited to, special, incidental, or other damages. Our views and rights are the same: You are responsible for your own choices, actions, and results. Permission should be addressed in writing to Johan Frederik Schuringa at expeditions@lifeworkproject.org

Editor: Debbie Sawczak

Layout & Design: Jeremy King - jeremy@lifeworkproject.org

Augmented reality licensed from UIM Insights Limited (www.pearlapp.ca)

ISBN 13: 978-1-989756-56-0

ISBN 10: 1989756565

BRING THIS BOOK TO LIFE THROUGH AUGMENTED REALITY

Hear personally from the author and experience key Bible scripture brought to life using your smartphone and the Pearl app. Watch for images with the vue icon and follow the instructions below.

Scan or search for "Pearl Lens" to download

Open app and scan image with lens

Content will load on your device for convenient viewing

Scan image to begin your LifeWork journey

Daniel Ramlogan with Joe Schuringa,
co-founders of the Lifework Project

CONTENTS

Starting out 9

1. What is it? 11
2. Credibility 13
3. Practise, Practise, Practise 16
4. Goals Unrealized 18
5. Slow Going 20
6. How to Lose a Business 22
7. An Owner's Attitude 25
8. "Can't" Thinking 27
9. Training: An Ongoing Process 29
10. Listening 31
11. Success Demands Change 33
12. Wishing and Dreaming 35
13. Entitlement 37
14. Know When to Let Go 39
15. Mistakes as Lessons 41
16. The Beauty of Duty 43
17. Discouragement 45
18. Your Anchor 47
19. Important? 49
20. The Winning Attitude 51
21. Enthusiasm 53
22. Trust 55
23. Persist...Or Else 57
24. Retirement 59
25. What Does It Take to...Win? 61
26. The Power of Assumption 63
27. The Difficult 65
28. Discipline 68
29. Setbacks 70
30. Failing is Part of Succeeding! 72
31. The Yabbut Disease 73
32. Team Building: The Way to Success 75
33. It's a Head Thing 77

34.	Standards	79
35.	Standing Out	81
36.	100 Percent Responsible	83
37.	Job Satisfaction	85
38.	Duty at work	87
39.	The Fixer	89
40.	Your Third Eye	92
41.	The Ideal	94
42.	Encourage	96
43.	Keep the Power On	98
44.	Stop and Reflect	100
45.	Life's Instructions	102
46.	Conflict in the Workplace	104
47.	Your Goodwill Account	107
48.	Essentials	110
49.	Maintenance	112
50.	Diligence	114
51.	Yielding: The Relational LUBRICANT	116
52.	What's in It for Me?	118
53.	The Power of Expectations	121
54.	Commitment	123
55.	How to Find Your Passion	125
56.	The Need to Add	128
57.	Potential	130
58.	Second Chance?	132
59.	Uphill	134
60.	Decisions	136
61.	Grow	140
62.	The Prayer of the Participant	142
63.	Work: A Burden, or a Delight?	144
64.	Being Steadfast	146
65.	Feelings, Unchecked	148
66.	There's a Price to Pay If...	150
67.	Talent	152

Acknowledgments 155
About the Author 157

STARTING OUT

Everywhere in life, life itself is waiting to surprise you. Gateways to splendour, the friends you wish you had, the wealth, security, family, and adventure you desire.

First you must believe it. Behind the darkness of many of your days, the dullness of work, the dragging yourself through drudgery, there's a world full of colour and wonder, if only you'll accept the invitation. If you do, you'll find yourself being remade, under the specifications of the original design, by the original Designer, in a collaborative project.

"Come, follow me," is the challenge—meaning not me, Joe Schuringa, but the one I've been following for quite some time now. And his command is: Be courageous.

This book is a collection of the weekly blogs I have been writing to my family and friends over the last few years. It contains the whole of the blogs as they were edited and published. It is meant to be a companion piece to the online form of these, which you'll find at the LifeWorkProject.org website.

Enjoy; I know I'll hear how you did, one fine day.

1

WHAT IS IT?

It's important for those who are in pursuit of success in the workplace that they know the answer to the question "What is it?" That is, what is it that turns your crank, what is it you are passionate about, what is it that turns you on? If your answer is "I don't know," or "There's really nothing," then success in the workplace or in any other field of endeavour will likely never get beyond the wishing stage.

There was a period in my life when my answer to the question "What is it? What are you passionate about?" was "Nothing, really." So I just kept drifting along like a piece of flotsam on the river of life—and that, dear reader, is truly a sorry state to be in.

So, what changed in my life to the point where, for 65 of my 86 years on this earth, lots of things have turned my crank, I am full of passion, and I became successful in most of the things I was passionate about? What happened? It began with a deep dissatisfaction with my directionless state, and the realization that unless I took action to bring about a change in my outlook and my life—action that included prayer—I'd continue to drift and be filled with self-pity as I watched others achieve and leave me behind.

I started by giving the job I had—but didn't like—outstanding effort. Before I knew it, my attitude changed and personal pride and confidence were born. Then my colleagues began to show me respect and I was promoted. A passion to excel took over, and I experienced the pride and elation that come from a job well done. From there, many other opportunities arose that turned my crank and lit my passion, the result of which has been some 65 years of having a reason to get up every morning and say, "Thank God for Monday morning and every morning," rather than just "Thank God it's Friday" at the beginning of the weekend, as in my days of drifting.

If you currently find yourself in the "I don't know" crowd and want to see this change, begin to give your all to the job you currently have, ask God's blessing on this new beginning, and watch yourself soar.

"But those who trust in the Lord will find new strength. They will soar high on wings like eagles. They will run and not grow weary. They will walk and not faint."
– Isaiah 40:31

2
CREDIBILITY

No one would argue that credibility is not vital to success in the business world, as well as any other honourable pursuit of our lives. I say "honourable" because I imagine that in a dishonourable venture, credibility may not weigh very heavily.

Success demands credibility, and credibility demands first of all that a person can be trusted. A person who cannot be trusted will find it impossible to achieve the credibility that is so vital to success. Credibility is only awarded to those whose word can be relied on, who will do what they say, who deliver on their promises, who represent the facts of a situation faithfully and don't shade the truth. Career advancement, business growth, healthy marriages, lasting friendships, etc. are all built on credibility.

But credibility demands other things as well. John Maxwell, a highly respected pastor, author, and motivational speaker, says this about credibility:

"To gain credibility, you must consistently demonstrate three things: Initiative: You have to get up to go up. Sacrifice: You have to give up to go up. Maturity: You have to grow up to go up. If you show the way, people will want to follow you. The higher you go, the greater the number of people who will be willing to travel with you."

Maxwell is talking about the things that invite respect as well as trust. People have high regard for those who are willing to take the first step to get things done, who will accept the costs and sacrifices necessary to achieve a goal, and who can set aside childish pettiness, stubbornness, and self-centredness.

Trustworthiness, initiative, sacrifice, and maturity: remember these things, apply them consistently, and watch your career, business, marriage, or other endeavour advance in direct proportion to your resulting credibility.

So how do we test our personal credibility? Here's a sure-fire test that will reveal where one stands on the credibility scale. For the result to be accurate, you have to be brutally honest with yourself in answering the following few questions. If you are married, ask or involve your spouse; otherwise, get a close friend to give input.

1. Do I take what I say, even such a small thing as "I'll meet you at ten" as a commitment, the kind I will keep short of an earthquake, or is it a loosey-goosey sort of thing where I may arrive at 10:15 or later or not at all?
2. Am I a "handshake" kind of person, the kind who would buy a car on a handshake? Or when push came to shove, would I back out, saying, "Well, I didn't sign for it!"
3. Do I trust my own promise, and would I be deeply disappointed in myself if I broke it?
4. Is my Yes a Yes, or is it really a Maybe? When I say Yes, am I determined to follow through?
5. Do other people trust me to deliver on my promises, and not to come back with reasons/excuses instead?
6. Do I give a truthful, straightforward account of things, even when it is to my disadvantage to do so, or do I shade the truth?

7. Do I by and large trust people, or is my attitude that "You can't trust anybody"?

Why this last question? Because we tend to see the world as we ourselves are. Not that we should be naïve; but if we generally expect trustworthiness from others, we are more likely to get it, and also to give it. Ultimately, our trust must be in God, whose credibility is total. He is the one who enables us to live in a way that invites others to trust us.

Trustworthiness, Initiative, Sacrifice, and Maturity—which add up to credibility—are assets no person or organization can afford to lose or do without. They are also traits that characterize the person who trusts in God.

> *"Trust in the Lord with all your heart; do not depend on your own understanding. Seek his will in all you do, and he will show you which path to take."*
> – Proverbs 3:5-6

3

PRACTISE, PRACTISE, PRACTISE

To win and to achieve success, you have to practise and practise and practise without letup. This is a recognized truth accepted by all athletes and sports teams looking to win and enjoy the rewards of winning. Most of us have no trouble accepting this truth as it applies to sports; we would respond with a contemptuous snort to a non-practising athlete who complained about losing: of course the person lost, because they never practised!

The fact is that "practise, practise, practise" applies not only to athletes but to all of us who are in pursuit of winning and reaping success in whatever endeavour we are engaged in—whether it be work, marriage, cultivating a positive attitude, overcoming a destructive habit, learning to walk in faith, or any other worthwhile pursuit. None of the above will happen unless we are determined and consistent in our practising!

So, what does this look like in a marriage, for example? Practising kindness and forbearance for a week or two won't achieve the success you crave; what's needed is ongoing practice that will eventually develop into a habit. Then you'll have a marriage that will be the envy of all who know you.

Similarly, if in the workplace you practise outstanding performance for a couple of weeks and expect immediate results, you'll be disillusioned and quit. It takes ongoing, determined practice and perseverance to develop a winning habit capable of delivering excellence at all times. Do this long enough, and you'll be a winner who is noticed and promoted.

You'll achieve success.

In my 86 years of life on this earth, 70-plus of these spent in the workplace and 40 as CEO of my own business, I have seen many people start with all kinds of good intentions, only to become discouraged and give up when the going got tough—as it inevitably does—and success was delayed. Such people fail to realize that they are forming a "quitting habit" which will inevitably lead to mediocrity at best, or outright failure at worst. And the really sad thing is that they'll then blame fate, their workplace, spouse, society at large, and often God for their lack of achievement, when all along it is their lack of persistent practice and determination to win—something fully within their control to remedy. Don't tell me that's not so! I know it is, for at one time in my life I was that guy.

Winning demands the cultivation of a winning attitude, and that takes practice, practice, and more practice. Yes, attitudes are developed—winning ones as well as losing ones. Athletes and sports teams that don't practise and practise with a winning attitude are doomed to lose, as are you and I if we do likewise.

I know you've heard it a thousand times before, but it's true: hard work pays off.

"If you want to be good, you have to practise, practise, practise."
– Ray Bradbury, author

"I am determined to keep your decrees to the very end."
– Psalm 119:12

4

GOALS UNREALIZED

You wouldn't start building a house whose plan lived only in your mind, would you? To do so would be rather foolish, don't you think? Most of us would want to get that mental picture of the home onto paper before starting to build. Unless we made a blueprint, with every detail drawn and priced—preferably in consultation with an engineer or architect—it's not likely the home would ever be completed.

It's like that with other goals and projects that live only in our minds: they'll likely never come to fruition unless they're written up in detail and discussed with people we trust, whose advice we value. Every goal needs a plan for how it will be achieved; what steps are going to be involved. And a goal or plan that is not written down is no more than a wish. It simply fades to nothing when the path to achieving it becomes difficult—as it almost certainly will, if the goal is worth anything. Furthermore, if you don't bounce your plans off some wise and experienced people, you risk attempting something unrealistic or ill-conceived.

So what's the answer if you want to see your goals come to fruition? A goal, to have a good chance of being realized, needs a fully written blueprint—a set of detailed plans—just like a house does. More than 95 percent of folk never blueprint their goals, and are therefore unable to calculate how much money, time, or effort it will take to make them happen. Nor do they seek advice. That's why so many people never see their goals realized.

Jesus said: "But don't begin [building] until you count

the cost. For who would begin construction of a building without first calculating the cost to see if there is enough money to finish it? Otherwise, you might complete only the foundation before running out of money, and then everyone would laugh at you." (Luke 14:28–29).

> *"Plans go wrong for lack of advice;*
> *many advisers bring success."*
> — Proverbs 15:22

5

SLOW GOING

Sometimes the progress in one's career is slow going, slow enough to trigger thoughts of quitting and looking for opportunities elsewhere. And though changing one's job is always an option—one which, after much careful thought and self-examination, could be the right one—this is not always the case. It could be that from the frying pan, you end up in the fire. The new job that promised so much may prove to be rather mundane or frustrating, offering even less opportunity than the one you just left.

What often happens in the career life of a dissatisfied employee is that the dissatisfaction produces a less-than-willing, lethargic work attitude, which in turn produces sloppy performance. All of this results in being overlooked when better opportunities and promotions do arise. After all, what supervisor or business owner would promote a slouch? Promotions and career progress go to the ambitious, the consistent hard workers, the ones with a "Can I help?" and a "What more can I do?" attitude.

In view of this, I recommend you do some careful, honest self-examination before you change jobs, as your slow progress may well be your very own fault. And if that proves true, you'll find the next job to be no better than the one you just left. We take ourselves with us wherever we go, so if you don't make a point of changing your ways, the attitude that caused the slow progress in one job will also cause slow progress in the next. A new attitude is needed to produce the progress you're after. And since that's the case, you might as well get on it right away: adopt the new attitude and new work ethic now, where you currently are, and see what happens. I venture to say that the pace of progress will pick up.

Why? Well, all workers are always being observed, by supervisors as well as co-workers, and when someone is an outstanding worker—or a mediocre one—word soon gets around. So when they observe you, what kind of a worker do they see? Ask yourself that question and give yourself an honest answer. Do they see a person who excels? If yes, then progress is pretty much guaranteed. This is what it says in Proverbs 22:29 (as paraphrased by Eugene Peterson in The Message): "Skilled workers are always in demand and admired; they don't take a backseat to anyone."

Evangelist Bob Gass says this: "Whether you realize it or not, you are being watched on the job. Your character, your work ethic, and your attitude are being observed. And you'll be rewarded not according to the tasks you complete, but for your attitude, and the way in which you complete them."

So, before you look for another job, examine yourself—your performance and attitude. If they need changing, change them! You'll soon see progress happen.

"Do you see a man who excels in his work? He will stand before kings; he will not stand before unknown men."
– Proverbs 22:29 (NK)

6
HOW TO LOSE A BUSINESS

It took me nearly 40 years to build a business that eventually employed some 80 people, and a little less than three to lose it. Let me share with you what I did that you should not do if you have a business.

The year was 1962 when I quit a job I liked—I mean really liked, so much that I couldn't wait for Monday morning to arrive so that I could go back to work. Although I was earning good money and able to provide for my wife and two-year old daughter—the first of three children—the promise of a new opportunity with the potential of doubling my income was just too much for me to pass up. So I accepted a franchise selling tire repair material to independent automotive repair garages, tire shops, and eventually car dealerships. The Lord blessed me with the ambition, determination, and stamina to build this one-man, one-truck operation to the point of employing the 80 people mentioned above.

Not that it was easy! Especially in the first few years, when my income dropped to less than half instead of doubling, we had a difficult time of it. And then when I started making money, it all had to go back into the business; since I hated borrowing, all expansion was self-financed. For about 20 years the traditional suppliers to the automotive trade (our competitors) referred to us contemptuously as "those wagon peddlers", and many bona fide wholesale suppliers to the trade refused to sell to us. So, yes, it was an uphill battle all the way.

How sweet the victory, then, when we finally grew to the point of building a 33 thousand-square-foot office and warehouse facility in a prestigious part of the city! At its opening, several of those very suppliers who had disdained us at first—and who were now supplying us—congratulated us on having brought "dignity" to our method of going to the market. The Lord continued to bless our efforts, and life was good.

Then when I was in my late 60s my general manager identified a promising market niche he suggested we take advantage of, so we did, and it proved to have a potential far beyond our most optimistic hopes and dreams. I was now approaching the age of 70, and we were advised that borrowing was justified to finance rapid expansion in order to capture this new segment of the market. Being a Grade 8 dropout, and never having borrowed, I felt uncomfortable and thought it prudent to hire a highly educated business grad with a master's degree as our new president.

Just short of three years later, this grad—wait for it—this grad had put the business into receivership. What, in hindsight, were my errors?

First, hiring someone who had no knowledge of our market or corporate culture. Second, agreeing to his request for autonomy, as a consequence of which I failed to monitor him. Third, trusting his promise that he would never let the company run short of money—a promise he failed to keep. Fourth, ignoring my gut feeling that I had hired the wrong guy and should fire him, though I eventually did so when it was too late. By then we had sunk from a healthy, debt-free company to a heavily debt-laden one, at the mercy of a bank demanding payment. We ended up in receivership.

What should I have done instead? If I were going to hire someone, it should have been a humbler person with some knowledge of our market. Alternatively, I should have promoted from within, as we had staff who knew the market and our culture, whom I could have sent to some business courses. I should also have set limits on our borrowing, slowed the expansion, and kept monitoring, monitoring, monitoring. And maybe some other things that you can think of.

So take a lesson from my experience, and don't make the same kinds of mistakes in your business. My mistakes were costly, but I learned from them, and God has allowed me to flourish again in their wake. "He who loses money loses much; he who loses a friend loses much more; he who loses faith loses all." Thankfully, my faith remained!

So, what do I do now? You'll find the answer to that at www.lifeworkproject.org.

7
AN OWNER'S ATTITUDE

There is such a thing as an attitude of ownership: an attitude of caring responsibility for property, for a business, or other resources, that typically characterizes the person who owns them. Noticing this, people often ask me which comes first: ownership, or the attitude of an owner? Do you develop the character and attitude of an owner after you own a home or business, or does the attitude come first and lead naturally to the fact of owning? Or is it a question of the chicken and the egg? Well, there is a bit of that here, because each does help to generate the other. But in this case I know the answer: the attitude of ownership comes first. How do I know this? I learned it in the university of life, through personal experience.

One will generally find a home or business owner to be a hardworking, caring, responsible, trustworthy, reliable, and self-disciplined person. Generally, they're not given to "that's-not-my-job" attitudes and behaviour. When they see something that ought not to be, they pitch in and do whatever it takes to make it the way it ought to be.

But it's those very characteristics in a person that result in home and business ownership in the first place! That's why you can and should have this responsible, caring attitude, which I call an "owner's attitude", even while working for someone else—because if you don't, you'll never end up owning a business or anything else of value. It takes a caring, responsible, trustworthy, reliable, self-disciplined, and hard-working person to get ahead in this world—to be promoted, to earn enough, and to save enough so that a business can be started or a home bought.

Jesus taught essentially the same principle in the parable of the servants: only those servants who had been trustworthy and hardworking with lesser responsibilities were deemed fit to receive greater ones.

The moral of the story? If you don't have an owner's attitude where you currently find yourself—a responsible, disciplined, hardworking attitude—then chances are you'll never be an owner. Clergyman and social reformer Henry Ward Beecher said, "Hold yourself responsible to a higher standard than anybody else expects of you; never excuse yourself." Do what Beecher says and you'll have a good chance of one day becoming an owner. You'll also feel good about yourself—and be on the receiving end of God's blessing.

"Well done, good and faithful servant. You have been faithful in handling this small amount, so now I will give you many more responsibilities. Let's celebrate together!"

– Matthew 25:21

8

"CAN'T" THINKING

Can you think of a word that stops progress and personal growth more effectively than "can't"? This word is a real killer. Let me give you a few examples of how this evil word does its destructive work.

"I can't change the way I think"—and you've just closed the door to advancement that demands a change in your thinking. "I can't do that job"—and you've just killed the desire to try something that might lead to a valuable new skill. "I can't do anything about the way I feel"—and you've just surrendered control of your thoughts to your fickle emotions. "That can't be done"—and you've just doomed the light bulb, the iPhone, the moonwalk, the airplane, heart and kidney transplants, even such a simple thing as the mousetrap: none of those were brought into being by "can't" thinkers, were they?

I could go on and on, but I trust you're getting the picture. Are you? It's sad indeed how often, perhaps without realizing it, we let the deadly virus of "can't" thinking enter our minds and poison our ambitions, hopes, and desires—not to mention our God-given potential to do and accomplish amazing things. The real kicker about "can't" thinking is that it prevents us from even starting a thing, because once you've told yourself it can't be done, there's obviously no point in even trying. "Can't" thinking is a close cousin to "what's the use?" thinking. Both leave you sitting in the dust of the can-do folk. Just remember that if you think "I can" or "I can't", you're always right.

What does it take to get out of this trap of "can't" thinking?

1. Admit you're in it.
2. Make up your mind to fight it.
3. Ask God to help you overcome it.
4. Trust him to do so.

Read what God says in Scripture, and "can't" thinking won't remain a problem in your life. And then watch your life change!

> *"'You have eyes—can't you see? You have ears—can't you hear?' Don't you remember anything at all?"*
> – Jesus (Mark 8:18)

9

TRAINING: AN ONGOING PROCESS

We all know and accept that athletes, to be any good, need to be involved in a regimented training program. We would consider foolish any athlete hoping to achieve a win or gain a medal without spending all kinds of time in an ongoing training program to perfect their skill. Even peewees in a hockey league have their practice and training time before the game to increase their chance of winning. They get expert instruction from their coach and then spend time applying it. We would be surprised if they didn't; we'd call their coach foolish or naïve.

But for some reason, we mostly don't apply this principle to ourselves and our work. All too often we expect progress and advancement without the extra time and effort needed to upgrade on an ongoing basis. And then when the desired advancement bypasses us, we complain or get angry, holding everyone else—often even God—responsible for our lack of progress.

It's kind of odd, isn't it, that we take for granted an athlete's need to train in order to win, but don't apply the same reasoning to our own expectations when it comes to workplace success. To expect to advance in the workplace without a personal training and upgrading program is as naïve and foolish as a gardener who believes plants will grow without being regularly watered.

Success in any field, including the workplace, demands the self-discipline of ongoing effort to sharpen and improve skills. Personal upgrades such as evening courses, online seminars, regular sessions with a mentor who has expertise in the field, or even a well-designed reading program, are a few examples of ways we can do this. And if you are a Christian, ongoing upgrading also includes the study of God's word, the Bible.

"Greatness is more than potential. It is the execution of that potential. Beyond the raw talent you need the appropriate training. You need the discipline. You need the inspiration. You need the drive."
– Eric A. Burns

"I discipline my body like an athlete, training it to do what it should. Otherwise, I fear that after preaching to others I myself might be disqualified."
– the Apostle Paul (1 Corinthians 9:27)

10

LISTENING

On a scale of 1 to 10, with 10 meaning "vital" and 1 meaning "of no importance", how would you rate listening? When I started out pursuing success I was told all kinds of things I needed to do, such as: get a good education, work hard, keep my nose to the grindstone, be determined —all of them true. Pay attention was also on the list, but rarely uttered with the same emphasis. Now, I was blessed with my share of victories and failures as the years passed, all of which eventually culminated in wonderful business success; but the journey would've been so much easier had I realized how vital listening is. You can't afford not to listen well, whether the success you're seeking is in a workplace or business setting or in a wholesome personal relationship.

Listening, really listening, doesn't come easily; it has to be learned. In fact, it's a very difficult skill to master or habit to develop. Listening is so much more than simply holding your tongue while the other party is talking. It's suppressing with all your mental power the urge to formulate your response while the other is speaking, and bending all that power instead to fully absorb and understand what the other person is saying. Half your brain cannot be busy with other things, with judging, weighing, or figuring out what you want to say. That only comes after. First, your whole attention must be occupied with taking in the other person's meaning. This takes extra time, which is why listening is not very popular in our culture where speed is an obsession.

Stephen Covey, in his book *The Seven Habits of Highly Successful People*, writes, "Seek first to understand."

Makes sense, doesn't it? Because how can you respond intelligently if you don't fully under-stand? And how can you understand without listening properly? Responding without fully understanding is what causes your spouse, child, employer, or co-worker to say, "He/she never listens!" If you're a quick-response person, you probably hear this quite often.

If you don't "seek first to understand", your poor listening will undermine success in all your relationships, and hence in your career. Without listening skills, you'll encounter many needless difficulties. Only late in life did I learn the importance of listening to understand; I would have been a much better leader, sales trainer, and leadership developer had I learned this lesson earlier.

So when, and how, should you respond? It goes without saying that you wait till the other person has stopped speaking. You might need several seconds to reflect on what you heard. Then you begin with, "Now, Joe, is this what you are saying?"—and restate what you heard the person say, that is, what you understood them to mean. What you think you heard is often not what the speaker intended. If you misunderstood, let them tell you again; if you got it right, you are now, and only now, ready to respond.

In this way you avoid misunderstandings, and create a kinship with the speaker: they will know and feel they were understood, contributing to relational growth. This skill does not come easily, so get started,

"Spouting off before listening to the facts is shameful and foolish."
– Proverbs 18:13

11

SUCCESS DEMANDS CHANGE

Success demands growth, and growth of any kind involves change! And if there's one thing the human being resists, being a creature of habit, it's change. All my experience tells me I am right in this; don't you agree? No doubt you've heard it said—and perhaps, at some time or other, have said it yourself: "I just can't change."

The unfortunate thing is that the ones with that mindset are heading for deep trouble in just about every facet of their lives: their career, the workplace, business in general, friendships, marriage, family relationships, their walk with the Lord.

All of the above, in order to be successful, demand ongoing adjustments and a willingness to change. We may need to change habitual ways of interacting, of responding to problems, of using our time and resources, of making decisions, or other behaviours. We may need to accept a change in roles and responsibilities, location, employment, or some other part of life. The ones who don't have this willingness to change will see their marriages break up, their relationships shipwrecked, their careers stagnate, and their walk with the Lord marred and eventually broken.

The "I just can't change" mindset is really an "I won't change" mindset, as everyone—when the will is there, and when God's help is invited and accepted—is capable of change. Someone with an I-won't-change attitude is like a tree that won't bend with the wind: it'll get snapped in two instead. Don't be like that tree.

Though change can be upsetting and uncomfortable

as well as difficult, the end result of positive, God-honouring change is always rewarding. Turning from an attitude of "I can't/won't change" to one of "I can and will change if growth demands it" will have God's blessing and produce miracles of success in careers, business, relationships, marriages, and most of all in your walk with the Lord. Take my word for it; it worked for me, and it'll work for you.

> *"A person with a changed heart seeks praise from God, not from people."*
> – Romans 2:29

12

WISHING AND DREAMING

The poet and essayist Dr. Samuel Johnson said, "The one who embarks on the voyage of life will always wish to advance rather by the impulse of the wind than the strokes of the oar; and many fold in their passage while they lie waiting for the gale."

I think what he's saying is that so many of us never get beyond the wishing, and I might add the dreaming, failing to realize that neither the wish nor the dream will ever become a reality unless the wisher and dreamer mans the oars and helps make it so.

Wishing and dreaming can be a pleasant pastime, but that's all it will do: pass the time. Before you know it, a big chunk of life will have passed with nothing accomplished. Then when you wake up from the dream—and there's always a wakeup—it is often too late to bring about what you wished for and dreamed about. And thus it is doomed to remain just a wish and a dream. How sad! So it's my hope that you can see the downside of wishing and dreaming and guard yourself against its potential deadly consequence.

Am I saying that one should not have wishes and dreams? Of course not! Without them, you will stagnate. However, in order to be successfully realized, a wish or dream must be transformed into a desire strong enough to become a plan—a specific plan that aims at a goal you are willing to suffer for, work for, discipline yourself for, and deny other wishes for. That's right: you may have to sacrifice some less worthwhile wishes for the big one that becomes your dream. So choose carefully!

You may recall that Martin Luther King, Jr. had a

dream—one that he shared with the world and then proceeded to work many years and eventually die for. And his dream did become a reality, bringing about much that was right and good.

It is my hope for you that if God gives you a good and worthy dream, you will turn it into a plan and a goal, and then man the oars and work at making it the reality it is capable of becoming.

> *"Commit your actions to the Lord,*
> *and your plans will succeed."*
> – Proverbs 16:3

13
ENTITLEMENT

This is how the dictionary defines "entitled": believing oneself to be inherently deserving of privileges or special treatment.

If you are among those who believe this about themselves, then you are also among those who will be facing great difficulty upon entering the real world, especially the workplace. Why? Because those in the grip of the entitlement disease are about as welcome with co-workers as ants at a picnic or a skunk in the backyard.

The unfortunate fact you will have to accept and get used to is that the real world is a competitive place where only those pulling their weight make headway, and the ones making headway aren't about to pull any deadweight up the success ladder in the form of people who consider themselves entitled to effort-free success. No sirree, each person has to make that climb on their own. You may get a leg up here and there, but by and large it's personal skill and effort that make the grade.

Given this, I can't help but wonder why there are so many young people with this "I have rights, I am entitled" chip on their shoulder. (I say "young people" not because I think the upcoming generation is particularly bad in this regard—after all, I started out with a similar attitude myself—but simply because most older people have already learned from experience that it won't work.) And why, in this so-called enlightened age, do so many educators and schools pass students who ought to be failed, as if there were a world out there that will continue to be that indulgent? There isn't a winning sports team in existence where an attitude of entitlement is accepted; it's all hard work, discipline, and cooperation that wins games, and team members who refuse are soon dropped. It's the same in the world of business and commerce.

Entitlement may have worked for the monarchs of old, or plantation owners in the days of slavery in the southern United States, but it has never worked for the average person like you and me. So if overindulgent parents and teachers are encouraging you to feel entitled to success, and are unable or unwilling to let you fail when such is called for, then you'll be facing the downside of this poor preparation as soon as you enter the real world: your entitled assumptions will explode in your face and you will fail, and fail hard. Adapt a disciplined lifestyle, make a wholehearted effort, and pull your own weight, otherwise you will meet failure in the workplace. The marketplace is a competitive world with no room for an attitude of entitlement!

OK, that's the world, which is inescapable. And what does the Christian's GPS (God's Positioning System), the Bible, say about all of this? It also makes no bones about the call to work industriously and pull your own weight:

> *"The Lord God took the man and put him in the Garden of Eden to work it and take care of it."*
> – Genesis 2:15

> *"For even when we were with you, we gave you this rule: 'The one who is unwilling to work shall not eat.'"*
> – 2 Thessalonians 3:10

14

KNOW WHEN TO LET GO

There's a popular song by Kenny Rogers called "The Gambler". It's about two derelict gamblers riding a railway boxcar, and one of them is giving the other some advice about what it takes to win at poker. He mentions that in a card game, "You've got to know when to hold 'em, know when to fold 'em, know when to walk away, and know when to run."

The same advice applies to those who have a dream they are pursuing, or a business idea they're launching, that doesn't quite fly as hoped. In many cases like this, more effort is expended and more money is poured into the venture to make it do what we want to see it do. But in some of these cases the gambler's advice about folding and walking away is exactly what needs to be applied.

To the visionary or entrepreneur, this is often just too difficult, and they keep flogging what turns out to be a dead horse—that is, an idea that the market is not buying. This refusal to fold and walk away is not only very stressful to the principals driving the enterprise, it's also very hard on the pocketbook. Letting a dream rule despite common business sense often results in family bank accounts being emptied at best, or personal bankruptcy at worst—never mind the family and relational stress, which can exact an even greater price than the monetary loss.

But how do you know? Aren't you supposed to press on and never give up? Well, that depends. The problem usually arises when entrepreneurial types have acted rashly on the assumption that whatever they plan or dream of will work. They haven't consulted others with knowledge and experience—or if they have, they've rejected all negative input No one is going to throw cold water on their idea! They haven't counted the cost, or identified any limits on what they're able to put in. Then when they forge ahead, they do so without setting deadlines for definite objectives, and without coming up with a Plan B in case those deadlines are not met. They haven't determined ahead of time under what conditions they should conclude that the idea is a non-flyer, nor have they established any way of regularly measuring and monitoring their success, so they don't know when they're floundering until they go belly-up.

But if you've done the proper consultation and preparation, counted the costs, set necessary limits on your endeavour, established measurements for its success, discussed positive and negative outcomes, and devised an alternative plan just in case, then you will know when it's time to abandon Plan A, and you'll be ready with Plan B. That's not the same as throwing in the towel just because things are tough; it's trying a different strategy based on good sense. And if Plan B's deadline rolls around with no improvement? Then be wise, and walk. Don't end up flogging a dead horse.

"Suppose one of you wants to build a tower.
Won't you first sit down and estimate the cost, to see if
you have enough money to complete it?"
– Jesus (Luke 14:28)

15

MISTAKES AS LESSONS

No one escapes making mistakes. They're just part of the human experience, right from infancy. We learn to walk by falling, and through many falls we learn how to avoid them. Skiing, skating, and bicycle riding are learned in a similar way. In all of these it was by recognizing our mistakes, and learning from them, that we mastered the skill—even if we couldn't, as children, articulate in words exactly what those mistakes were. In other words, the mistakes we made became lessons that taught us how to avoid a painful repetition. Because we were so intent on mastering the skill, we didn't allow these mistakes to put us off or make us give up; we didn't treat them like failures but like stepping stones to success, which is exactly what they were.

How is it that when we grow older, we lose this wisdom of our youth? Somewhere along the line, we stop experiencing mistakes as lessons that teach us how to avoid repeating them. Of course, mistakes that are not identified and remembered are of no use; they'll only be repeated and produce the same pain all over again. It's only when we recognize and remember our mistakes, and make a point of learning something from them, that they can contribute to the success we're seeking. Let me give a few examples.

I was asked to be present as a consultant at a corporate five-year planning session attended by the corporation's leadership. A wonderful PowerPoint presentation showed all kinds of well-drawn graphs and colourful charts indicating anticipated profits and expansion. Feeling that something was missing, I asked for a list of the mistakes made during the last couple of years. I received no such list, only surprised and questioning looks.

Was it because no mistakes had been made? No; it was because they were not thought to play any kind of positive role in planning future growth. I explained that failure to clearly identify their past mistakes would lead to the likelihood of repeating them, and that it was well worth the time to identify those made during the past year or two as well as the costs associated with them.

When they did so, the value of the exercise became obvious to them. In going back over the mistakes and the resulting costs, the corporate leaders realized that no action had been taken to avoid a repeat, and that doing so could add substantially to growth and profits in the years to come.

Inattention to mistakes in relationships is the reason we keep making the same ones over and over, resulting in the breakup of marriages and other partnerships and friendships. Mistakes unidentified will be repeated; mistakes recognized, acknowledged as such, apologized for, and accompanied by the resolve not to repeat them become lessons that produce needed change, which in turn produces the success we are in pursuit of.

Football coach Paul Bryant says: "When you make a mistake, there are only three things you should ever do about it: admit it, learn from it, and don't repeat it."

> *"I applied my heart to what I observed,
> and learned a lesson from what I saw."*
>
> – Proverbs 24:32

16

THE BEAUTY OF DUTY

We don't often hear the word "duty" in connection with the workplace. In fact, the word "duty" is hardly ever used anywhere anymore in everyday life, including in the home. When was the last time you told your children they had a duty to perform certain tasks? When was the last time you were told at work that you had a duty to strive to excel, or told one of your workers they had a duty to do a full day's work for a full day's pay? If people say this sort of thing at all, they're more likely to use the word "responsibility". Talk of duty is going a bit far in the direction of fusty, dreary, regimented moralism. A bit old-fashioned. It might be appropriately applied to soldiers; but ordinary citizens?

Let me define what I'm talking about when I say "duty" as opposed to "responsibility" (another good word, but different). Duty, it seems to me, is something you absolutely have to do; responsibility is something you ought to do. There's no option about duty: you're either doing it or you aren't, and if you aren't, there's simply no excuse. It's just plain bad. But when it comes to responsibility, there seems to be a bit of wiggle room. Those who don't carry out their responsibilities we call "irresponsible"—lower on the scale than a responsible person, sure, but maybe just weaker in character; a C instead of an A. What do we call someone who doesn't do their duty? There's a difference, isn't there? Duty shouldn't be thought of as fusty, dreary, or outdated. It's sharp and clear, all or nothing, and describes the best and highest of timeless obligations.

As a Christian I believe that God is asking me and you

to think in terms of duty when it comes to worshiping him and obeying his commands. We are to think in terms of duty when it comes to our marriage vows, the care of our children, and the work and service we do for others—whether it's coming to the aid of a neighbour in distress, or the everyday work of our jobs or businesses. Duty leaves us no options; it's black and white, and there's no misunderstanding it. We're either doing it or not. Furthermore, our understanding of duty is what makes our specific responsibilities clear to us: they flow from our fundamental duty.

And the great thing is, when we do our duty, beautiful things result: good, strong relationships, excellence in the workplace, healthy self-respect, peace with God, and a deep-down contentment that will withstand hardship. That's why I've titled this article "the beauty of duty".

> *"That's the whole story. Here now is my final conclusion: fear God and obey his commands, for this is everyone's duty."*
> – Ecclesiastes 12:13

17

DISCOURAGEMENT

Discouragement is experienced by all of us who are pursuing a worthy objective, whether as a young child trying to master riding a bike, a student working towards a diploma, a man or woman striving to further their career, a business person competing in the marketplace, or a couple seeking happiness in their marriage.

In early childhood—when learning to eat with a spoon, say—our response to failure and parental encouragement is often one of frustrated anger, manifested by crying and throwing the spoon. This response is not the result of conscious thought but of emotion that boils to the surface involuntarily. Usually, it's not the determination of the young child but the ongoing encouragement of a caring adult that ultimately leads to the mastery of eating without spilling.

Unfortunately, some of us have not outgrown the childish spoon-throwing reaction to difficulties; we let feelings rule rather than thought. I've been there, so I know what I'm talking about. I've found that anger, crying, and spoon-throwing don't help to resolve a discouraging difficulty; they simply exacerbate it, producing more feelings of discouragement. Here's the grown-up cure:

- Get a piece of paper and write the problem down, as well as your thoughts on how or why it is triggering the gloomy feeling(s). This forces you to reflect and get some perspective.
- Share it with someone and ask for help or advice.
- Develop one or more action steps to tackle the

problem in a fresh way.
- Ask God's blessing on your action steps, and do them.

You'll be amazed at the results. Let me share a couple of personal experiences with you.

Discouraged by ongoing marital difficulties, I used to withdraw—or sulk, as my wife called it—feeding the anger and hurt and entrenching the feelings of discouragement. When I wrote the problem and understood how it triggered discouragement, shared it with somebody, asked for advice, and prayed about it, I came up with the solution: quit sulking, put the problem on the table, talk it over with my spouse, and get counselling. I did those things, and it worked!

Another time, discouraged by an overwhelming business problem, I felt helpless and defeated. My feelings said, "What's the use? Give up." I almost did; but then, using my head instead of being guided by my feelings, I resorted to the method described above: writing and identifying, sharing and asking for advice, coming up with actions to address the problem, and praying while carrying them out. I and those who helped me were able to defeat discouragement and replace it with renewed hope and positive action, which produced continued corporate growth.

Very often, until you write it down—which requires reflection—you can see only the problem that feeds the discouragement, not its source or the solution that defeats it.

"Why, my soul, are you downcast? Why so disturbed within me? Put your hope in God, for I will yet praise him, my Saviour and my God."
— Psalm 42:5

18

YOUR ANCHOR

There's a hymn I really like that asks: "Will your anchor hold in the storms of life?" We all know that the storms of life—difficulties and trials—affect us all, without exception. At one time or another, we all find ourselves on the receiving end of such as these. There's just no escaping the storms of life, is there?

So why am I quoting a hymn in a blog about success in one's career and life in general? It's because your success—in the workplace, your career, marriage, and personal development—is closely tied to whatever value system anchors you. A ship anchored on a sandy bottom will have its anchor drag when the storm hits, and will end up shipwrecked. It's like that with you, too, when difficulties come your way (and they will come!), such as the loss of your business or your job, the death of a loved one, the breakup of your marriage or other relationship, serious illness, or any other unexpected hardship.

Is your value system, your faith, able to withstand the setbacks, deal with the difficulties, and help you overcome? Or will you despair, cave in, and give up? Will you accept the opportunity to grow and become stronger, or will you blame God, society, your parents, or some other culprit? Will you move on to restoration, peace, and renewed confidence, or will you adopt a "what's the use" attitude? The answer to this depends on how well you are anchored.

The hymn I mentioned has a refrain that provides an answer to the question posed in the first line. This is what it says, and this is what's available to all of us:

"We have an anchor that keeps the soul Steadfast and sure while the billows roll, Fastened to the Rock which cannot move, Grounded firm and deep in the Saviour's love."

When you are anchored to this Rock, the Rock that cannot move, you'll be able to handle whatever lifestorm you find yourself in. You'll be able to deal with whatever setbacks, discouragements, trials, or difficulties come your way. You might be thinking, "That's easy for you to say, Joe, but if you had my problems you'd talk differently." Maybe, but I did have my marriage break up, and last year celebrated my 60th year of marriage to the woman who walked out. I lost many jobs and yet was able to build a successful business for 40 years. And then I lost that business, and thought that at age 76 I'd sit on the ashes of despair. Instead I'm blessed with starting and running a seminar (now at age 86) on the Christian and Success in the Workplace.

I'm convinced this came about because I was and am anchored to the Rock that cannot move. It's this Rock that helped me deal with life's storms and overcome whatever damage they managed to inflict. And it's this Rock that will do the same for you. Try him, and you'll find it's true.

"Consider it pure joy, my brothers and sisters, whenever you face trials of many kinds, because you know that the testing of your faith produces perseverance. Let perseverance finish its work so that you may be mature and complete, not lacking anything."
— James 1:2-4

19

IMPORTANT?

"Important" is a word that is often abused, with the result that it loses much of its punch. The word is abused when an impatient person uses it to get someone else to do something in a hurry when in reality the task did not demand that kind of immediate action. Of course, it's important to do all work well and in a timely fashion. We shouldn't procrastinate. But neither should "it's important!" be used to manipulate someone into setting aside some other task in order to do what we want. Do this often enough, and "important" loses its significance—which is tragic, as people then fail to believe it when it is used of things that truly are important. Sound familiar? It's like the boy who cried "Wolf!"

In a workplace where bosses, supervisors, and colleagues have a tendency to overuse this word to spur others to action, they'd better understand that it will lose its power—just as a much-used knife will grow dull and lose its cutting ability. And when that happens, nobody can tell what's really important.

So, for a Christian in pursuit of career advancement or business growth, what's the truly important thing to keep in mind in order to see such endeavours succeed? Our spiritual GPS, the Bible (God's Positioning System), provides us with clear directions on that:

"Whatever your hand finds to do, do it with all your might" (Ecclesiastes 9:10). Here we're told that it's important to put our whole heart into our work, to strive to excel at what we are asked to do every working day. Another Scripture says, "Whether you eat or drink or whatever you do, do it all to the glory of God" (1

Corinthians 10:31). So every morning on the way to work, it is important to commit our day to the Lord and ask him for his help: "Help me, Lord, to honour you in the work I do today. I offer it to you."

God's Word also tells us that when we walk in obedience to his directives, he will bless our efforts. Don't misunderstand; this is not a prosperity gospel. The blessing of God is not necessarily wealth and the granting of all our wants and wishes. Rather, his blessing is joy and satisfaction in our work; it is courage and peace even in difficult and stressful circumstances; it is a sense of meaning and purpose; good relationships with others; and delight in sharing God's pleasure with what we have done. These are all important ingredients for a happy life.

It is important to remember the Law of the Farm. The farmer who prays for a blessing on his crops cannot receive it if he does not do his part—the work involved in planting, tending, and harvesting. God says to the farmer, and to you and me: "Give me something to bless." You and I need to work as unto the Lord, with all of our might, so that God can bless our efforts. That is the most important thing to remember about success.

> *"You will eat the fruit of your labour;*
> *blessings and prosperity will be yours."*
> – Psalm 128:2

20
THE WINNING ATTITUDE

Which attitude leads to career and business success, as well as most other honourable achievement? The one I believe to be most important to success is often not a part of the initial planning and goal-setting process. This oversight is the primary contributing factor in not seeing the desired result produced—be it a flourishing business, a rising career, a new invention, or an educational achievement. Most ambitious men or women give little thought to how anyone else might benefit. They're focused on personal gain: what's in it for me? It's a self-centred attitude.

For the Christian striving to live according to God's directives—the highest being love your neighbour—this is a serious mistake. The importance of thinking of the needs of others is not just for Christians; any common-sense business owner knows that he or she had better run a business to the genuine benefit of customers and employees (as well as self), or it will fail. Where customer and employee benefits are not top priority, a business will soon see customer loss and unacceptable employee turnover, both of which spell disaster for any company in pursuit of growth and lasting profit. With a me-first, bottom-line-only mentality, corporate growth and longevity are about as likely to materialize as snow in July.

Few people would quarrel with customer and employee benefits being vital to a lasting and growing business or career, but many somehow think these can be a lower priority in the very beginning of one's planning and goal setting, presumably because all the focus has to be on simple survival: getting out of the gate and accumulating capital. Only then do we turn our attention to maximizing benefit for customers and employees. But this is a misconception. If benefit for others is not in our sights when we have little, it won't be there when we have much. Jesus said, "Whoever is faithful in little is faithful also in much; and whoever is unjust in small things is also unjust in greater things" (Luke 16:10). In other words, the me-first attitude does not diminish, but tends to grow stronger as we get more.

To reap God's blessings on your plans, and growth in business, you had better be one who focuses on how others can benefit. The famous inventor Edison, when working on the light bulb, wasn't primarily thinking about how much money he'd be making, but rather about how much people would benefit from his replacement for the candle and how it would improve people's lives. Someone once said, "It is our attitude at the beginning of a difficult task—which includes the setting of goals—that will affect its successful outcome more than anything else."

Now, maybe you're not an entrepreneur. How does this principle apply to career advancement? Glad you asked! The best and fastest way to see your career advance is with a how-can-I-help, what-more-can-I contribute attitude. This attitude spells success for self and for others—your colleagues and your company—and it pleases God.

> *"Don't look out only for your own interests,
> but take an interest in others, too."*
> – Philippians 2:4

21

ENTHUSIASM

Here's a question for you: What role does enthusiasm play in achieving success in any field, be it the workplace, your career, ministry, business, charity, marriage, or whatever?

The answer is simple: it plays a vital role! Enthusiasm is as vital to achieving happiness and success in any endeavour as oil is vital to the running of an engine, or water to the effective use of a bar of soap. Try washing yourself with only a bar of soap and no water. It's like that also when trying to achieve worthy goals without enthusiasm. It just won't happen. Your heart has to be in it, you have to be eager, and you have to believe it's possible. That's what enthusiasm is.

Unfortunately, though, enthusiasm isn't something we are born with: It must be developed. It needs to be planted, and then nurtured continuously, like a fire needs to be lit and then fed to keep burning. So how does one develop enthusiasm? The only way I know of is to keep your eye on the DRP, which stands for the Desired Result that you want to see Produced; in other words, the end result, the goal.

Let me give you a simple example. I was the president of the company and always came to work early. One morning on my way through the warehouse to my office I saw a mess of half-picked orders, cluttered aisles, packing materials all over the place, and so forth. All I could think was how depressing it was to come in to a workplace like this. What a lousy start to a working day! And how enthusiasm-draining! So I gathered up a bunch of brooms and mops (also sold by our company) and placed them by the entry door. As our employees came in, I shared with them my reaction to the warehouse mess, and I could see that most, if not all, felt as I had: depressed by it.

I then asked, "Would you like to leave work every day feeling good about what you achieved that day, good about what you had left behind you, and good about coming in the next day to a well-organized and clean workplace?" The response was unanimous: they would all like that! I then handed out the brooms, and all of us—me included—started sweeping, cleaning, and organizing the place. It took us half an hour.

What is to be noted here is that it was done with enthusiasm, as they could visualize the end result, a result that they desired: a clean and organized workplace instead of a demoralizing, messy one. And it was an activity whose result generated more enthusiasm: for the next 30 years that I was president, time was taken every day to clean and organize before quitting so that people could come in the next day with pleasure and get straight to work in an environment conducive to continued enthusiasm.

Can a simple task of sweeping be done enthusiastically? Yes, it can, if the sweeper's DRP (Desired Result to be Produced) is the cleanest warehouse in the park, worthy of praise and feeling good about, and if the sweeper visualizes and believes in that DRP.

> *"Enthusiasm spells the difference between mediocrity and accomplishment."*
> – Norman Vincent Peale

> *"Work with enthusiasm, as though you were working for the Lord rather than for people."*
> – Ephesians 6:7

22

TRUST

What role do you think trust plays in the workplace? How important is trust to the success of your own career and the success of your company? How would you define trust, and what does it look like in your life? Are you one of those—there seem to be quite a few of them—who trust nobody, or are you one who—foolishly, some say— trusts everybody?

I hope you belong to the trusting group, as trust (or the lack of it) plays a vital role in workplace and career success (or failure). Here's something to be noted: how much you trust other people has more to do with your own character than theirs. In other words, we see the world as we are. In my nearly 70 years in the workplace (40 as CEO of my own business), I've generally found that the trustworthy trust and the unreliable and untrustworthy don't.

Here are a few comments and observations on trust by some well-respected folk:

> *"One must be fond of people and trust them if one is not to make a mess of life."*
> – E. M. Forster, author

> *"I think we may safely trust a good deal more than we do."*
> – Henry David Thoreau,
> American essayist, poet, and practical philosopher

> *"Our distrust is very expensive."*
> – Ralph Waldo Emerson,
> preacher, essayist, lecturer, philosopher

> *"You may be deceived if you trust too much, but you will live in torment unless you trust enough."*
> – Frank Crane, Presbyterian minister, speaker, and columnist

To be successful in one's career and in the building of a business it's essential to trust and be trustworthy, because none of us can be and do everything we need, and none of us can verify everything in advance: at some point each of us must rely on others, proceed on goodwill, and make decisions based on unguaranteed information. As I've made clear in other blog posts, there is no success without risk, including interpersonal risk—and risktaking requires trust.

If you currently work in an environment where leadership and co-workers don't trust one another, I would suggest you look for another job, as neither the workers, the management, nor the business will be going places other than downhill.

> *"Commit everything you do to the Lord.*
> *Trust him, and he will help you."*
> – Psalm 37:5

> *"Do for others just what you want them to do for you."*
> – Luke 6:31

23

PERSIST...OR ELSE

Persist: what a beautiful word, a word that holds such great promise! However, its promise is only realized if it's lived, especially when the inevitable difficulties arise in one's pursuit of success—be it in education, one's career, the workplace in general, marriage and family, spiritual life, or any other area. On the way to every worthwhile goal, obstacles are guaranteed; so if you're aiming to succeed, there had better be a little voice in your mind that keeps on shouting, "Persist!" Otherwise, failure is guaranteed!

Thomas Carlyle, a well-known writer, historian, and teacher, said this: "Permanence, perseverance, and persistence in spite of all obstacles, discouragements, and impossibilities: it is this that in all things distinguishes the strong soul from the weak."

To succeed in anything worthwhile, persistence is required. Its absence is particularly evident in the way some people set or announce their worthy goals, and is the reason that so many good intentions never get off the runway. "I hope to achieve such-and-such" is the kind of statement that signals lack of persistence; a person who merely hopes to achieve a particular goal has a desire to succeed, but is already silently and unintentionally accepting potential failure. That person has no commitment to achieve, is likely to give up when obstacles arise, and will excuse the resulting failure by saying something like, "Well, I had hoped to, but it didn't happen." Since there was no acceptance of responsibility to succeed in the first place, there is also none when failure results, and hence no lesson is learned that will produce future success.

By contrast, the committed person, the one who plans to persist in the face of whatever difficulties he or she encounters, says, "I will achieve such-and-such." "I will persist" is a statement of commitment, of refusal to give up, and this is the attitude that produces the miracles of success in any realm of life.

It takes tremendous courage to make this kind of positive statement. But unless you do, winning is a very remote possibility. If you are a Christian and you think this kind of statement is too bold to receive God's blessing, I suggest you read the Psalms. There you'll see a lot of "I will" and "I shall" statements.

It was persistence that produced the light bulb, it was persistence that produced penicillin, the polio vaccine, the vote for women, flight, and countless other blessings. It is persistence that brings an ordinary person to a diploma and the necessary knowledge and skill set to be a medical doctor. And it will be persistence in setting worthy goals for you and your family, and persistence in pursuing these goals despite difficulties, that will produce a better marriage, paycheque, business, or career. Persistence is what will result in stronger faith, greater courage, and deeper peace in your inner being. These will be God's gifts to you, if you seek Him in setting your goals and then persist in pursuing them.

"Let us run with perseverance the race marked out for us, fixing our eyes on Jesus, the pioneer and perfecter of our faith."
– Hebrews 12:1, 2

24

RETIREMENT

Sooner or later the thought of retirement comes up in our minds—in fact, these days it often seems to be sooner rather than later: believe it or not, I've heard many talk about retiring in their early fifties, or even earlier. Notably, when these retirement thoughts come up they generally seem to trigger visions of utopia. Yes, we can hardly wait for the paradise of retirement! Travelling, seeing the world, lying on the beach, sleeping in, making spur-of-the moment visits to friends and family—at last, the chance to do as we please! No more dull routine! No more rat race! Heavenly freedom from the workplace call of duty, taxing our brain and demanding our time and energy. Retirement can't come soon enough!

But when the longed-for retirement arrives, in some cases as early as one's fifties, many of us find after a year or two that utopia isn't all it was cracked up to be. It can be much like the experience of a starving person who eagerly looks forward to a nourishing meal: once satisfied, the yearning is gone and any more would make us sick.

When does this disappointing realization dawn on the retiree? When we find that without the demands, duties, and stresses of work, we no longer have a reason to get up in the morning. It begins shortly after we discover that we're not needed anymore, that spur-of-the-moment visits are not much appreciated by friends and family, that sleeping in is not half as satisfying as it was when we worked, that cruises are eating up too much retirement money, and that lying on beaches is really not that great and can in fact become boring. The excitement we felt about an upcoming holiday when we were working has disappeared.

Disillusionment sets in when we wake up and have to ask ourselves, "Now what will I do today?"—and nothing pressing or challenging comes to mind. Letdown sets in when we realize that whether we do or don't do whatever does come to mind, it doesn't really matter. We begin to experience dissatisfaction when the energy of a person still under 70 years of age demands to be expended, and the God-given talents demand to be used, and there's nothing to focus them on. We begin to yearn for the responsibilities we once found so boring, the challenges we once resented, and a few of the workplace problems that stimulated our intellect, of which we still have so much unused.

I guess you get my point, all you who are yearning for retirement: it's not the utopia it's cracked up to be. Here's my advice if you're not yet 65, or even if you're older and still have your strength: replace your longing for retirement and idleness, for doing only what you feel like doing, with a healthy dose of gratitude for the job you now have, with all its pressures and challenges.

And when you do retire, find some other worthwhile kind of work to do that will use your gifts and skills to benefit others and keep you engaged and alert. May you be blessed like me (I'm 86) and counted among those the psalmist is talking about when he says:

> *"Even in old age they will still produce fruit;*
> *they will remain vital and green."*
> – Psalm 92:14

25

WHAT DOES IT TAKE TO...WIN?

Good question, don't you think? It's a question that has doubtless been asked by most people at one time or another, especially when running into seemingly insurmountable obstacles and unanticipated difficulties while striving to win at something that is important to them. At such times we may well cry out, often in desperation, "What does it take to win?"

Hundreds if not thousands of books have been written on the subject of winning and succeeding, so what can this little blog add to that? A few simple pointers to help, especially if you're struggling, to get back on track and continue to walk the path towards the "win" you're in pursuit of—in your workplace, marriage, relationship, studies, business, freedom from addiction, or other area.

I have found that winning begins with dissatisfaction: the dissatisfaction with what is; which seeds a desire for change. This desire needs to be strong enough to trigger an action plan consisting of the steps you need to take to see the change realized. A desire that doesn't trigger an action plan is just a wish, and will go nowhere. To generate a plan of action, the desire has to be powerful and passionate.

Once you've formed an action plan in your mind, be sure to commit it to paper and bounce it off some folk you trust for their input and advice—and don't forget to ask God for his wisdom and guidance in the matter. This step of committing your plan to paper is crucial, though unfortunately often neglected. Sure, there are a few people who, by chance, do achieve their goal using a plan strictly in their head; however, a written plan will do for you what the blueprint does for a builder. It's more likely to succeed.

Next, imagine the difficulties you may have to deal with, and make a list of them. You may need the input of other experienced people to help you with this, too. Why identify difficulties ahead of time? To be prepared when they inevitably arise. Be sure you come up with a backup strategy for each difficulty you identify.

Finally, make a decision to proceed and to stay the course despite challenges; and share this decision with everybody who counts in your life. Why? Because it'll help you hang in when the difficulties and roadblocks start screaming, "It won't work, you're in over your head, so give up!" You won't want to admit failure to all those with whom you've shared your decision, those who matter to you; you won't want to disappoint their hopes for you. Besides, if they know about your decision, they can encourage and support you. But if nobody knows what you were after, it's easier to just quit.

Take these simple steps and hang in there; winning is within your reach.

"Success is almost totally dependent upon drive and persistence. The extra energy required to make another effort or try another approach is the secret of winning."
– Dennis Waitley

"David continued to succeed in everything he did, for the Lord was with him."
– 1 Samuel 18:14

26

THE POWER OF ASSUMPTION

For most of my 40-year business career I was CEO of my own business and the corporation's main sales trainer. During this period I saw a lot of sales never closed, and a lot of sales careers bite the dust, due to negative assumptions. The same habit was responsible for careers that either never got off the ground, or if they did, flew no higher than the treetops. These poor lollypops (the Christian word for suckers) were ruled by the habit of making negative assumptions. For example, they'd approach a potential customer with the assumption, "I just know this customer will never buy," and then prove the assumption true by never asking for the order! When this success-destroying habit takes hold in a person's thinking, it almost always leads to failure or at best mediocrity. Barring the odd exception, it sure did in my business, and does so in many sales careers that run aground.

But it's not confined to sales. Take a look at yourself and your pursuit of success in whatever field or endeavour you are currently engaged in, and reflect on how your assumptions are at work in determining your actions. Are your assumptions mostly positive, or mostly negative? When setting out on a new venture, do you assume that given the necessary investment of time, resources, and effort, you'll succeed? Or do you think, "Well, I'll give it try, but I'm not all that confident of success." If your marriage is in a valley at the moment, do you assume it'll never get any better? Or do you think, "If I make up my mind to change my behaviour, and ask for God's help, of course it'll get better!" Do you assume failure, or do you assume success?

I don't know how old you are, but if you're young and want to do something bold, do you expect success in spite of your young age, or do you figure nobody will listen to you because you're just too young? What about you older people? Do you assume your time is past because you're too old? Or do you assume that, like Moses who was called at age 80, you can still be used by God to work in his kingdom? Your actions and ultimate success in any endeavour will be determined in no small measure by your assumptions. There's a direct correlation: negative assumptions -> negative results; positive assumptions -> positive results. As Laurie Mayers, a successful entrepreneur and author, says: "Don't build roadblocks out of assumptions."

Jesus has a word that may help you see a positive result rather than a negative one when it comes to prayer. "Therefore, I tell you, whatever you ask for in prayer, believe that you have received it, and it will be yours" (Mark 11:24). Amazing, isn't it? But when you pray, always make sure that what you're asking for is God-honouring and God-pleasing; if you sincerely ask yourself whether it is, you'll know the answer in your heart of hearts. And be prepared to wait for God's timing. I felt God's call to start a seminar dealing with Christians and Success in the Workplace, and assumed I'd be successful in that endeavour; but I had to keep trusting and working for ten years before finally, at age 85, I was able to do it.

So, in all endeavours, assume the best; but be prepared to hang in there, make a consistent wholehearted effort, be patient, pray, believe in God's answer, and accept God's timing.

27

THE DIFFICULT

Scott Peck, in The Road Less Traveled, says, "Life is difficult. This is a great truth. It is a great truth because once we truly see this truth, we transcend it. Once we truly understand and accept it—then life is no longer difficult. Because once it is accepted, the fact that life is difficult no longer matters."

Life is always difficult—very difficult, in fact, especially for those who think it ought not to be so; for those who understand and accept that life is difficult, the fact is less upsetting. The key here is acceptance. If we go through life thinking it should be easy, that it is in fact easy for everyone else except me, then life is indeed difficult, and bitter complaint seems justified. It's only by accepting life's inherent difficulty that we can diminish its power and importance in our lives.

I started my working career at age 15 in farming, and soon discovered that the farming life was difficult. Not wanting a difficult life, I left farming, seeking success and an easier life. This search—carried out while complaining all the time about my difficult life—lasted about seven years and produced some 40 career changes. Not till my early twenties (I'm now 86) did I finally understand that there was no easy life, and that I'd better dig in if I wanted to meet with some measure of workplace success. So I did, and eventually reaped the blessings that go hand in hand with hard work and a job well done. I was able to start my own business, and was blessed with more than 40 years of business success. It was during these years that I learned to accept that life was difficult, thereby obviating the need to complain. What changed? An accepting attitude—of course there's difficulty, so deal with it—helped me face and get through the difficulties without self-pity. It made life so much easier and enjoyable.

If you are currently among the many who refuse to understand and accept that life is difficult, you're likely unhappy with the work you have, always looking for that perfect job elsewhere, only to find that it ain't there. Maybe you've heard people talk about their jobs with such pleasure and enthusiasm, you imagine they don't encounter any difficulty. But everyone does! The people who love their work have just learned to accept and deal with those difficulties.

The person who can't accept that life in general is difficult, and gets upset when difficulties come, can be compared to a car mechanic who gets upset about grease on his hands and clothes, or a gardener getting upset over weeds in her garden. Pretty silly! Clearly the best way for them to avoid frustration and upset is to accept grease on clothes and weeds in garden as normal, and just deal with it when it happens.

It's like that with relationships and marriages, too. You'd better understand and accept that neither will be easy but often difficult; then you won't be blindsided by the difficulty when it comes. You'll say "of course!" and simply take it in stride, deal with it, and overcome.

A wise person named J. Donald Walters once said:

"Self-acceptance comes by meeting life's challenges vigorously. Don't numb yourself to your trials and difficulties, nor build mental walls to exclude pain from your life. You will find peace not by trying to escape your problems and difficulties, but by confronting them courageously. You will find peace not in denial, but in victory."

In a similar vein, in my company we used to have a slogan on our wall that read, "The difficult we do right away; the impossible takes a little longer." With that kind of attitude, life can become an exciting adventure with victory upon victory.

The Bible tells us in Psalm 118 that "Songs of joy and victory are sung in the camp of the godly." Strive to be in that camp, and you'll be able to deal with life that's difficult.

28

DISCIPLINE

Discipline! That most vital and essential ingredient in all achievement and success. It's a word that likely triggers thoughts of your youth, where parental discipline—if you were lucky enough to have parents who disciplined—set the standards, and your obedience to those standards was enforced by means of whatever system of reward and punishment your parents used.

This memory may not be very pleasant for you. But then you grew up and left your home, and parental discipline was no longer there to set boundaries for you or to guide you. It's a transition that ends badly for some, who go hog-wild and behave in a most undisciplined manner, as often seen in the lives of first-year university students.

Fortunate indeed are those who wake up from this self-indulgent and destructive lifestyle and learn to practise self-discipline—because that's what is needed if they want to be counted among the successful achievers in life. The ones who never graduate from parental discipline to self-discipline are left behind in the valley of mediocrity, failure, and envy, never to see the world from the mountaintop. I know what I'm talking about, because for several years after escaping parental discipline I was one of those undisciplined people, living a self-indulgent life that brought me no lasting pleasure. I ended up standing frustrated on the sidelines, watching the disciplined folks achieve success in the workplace, their relationships, their earnings, their self-respect, their personal confidence and pride.

Like the prodigal son in the parable Jesus told, I only came to my senses when I found myself up to my neck in the pig-poo of failure. I asked God to help me cultivate some self-discipline so I could get out of the hole and begin to climb the success mountain. All you need to climb this mountain, impossible though it may seem at times, is self-discipline, determination, and a never-say-die attitude. With God's help I was able to develop these, and the result was the material and relational success I craved. I was able to start and build a flourishing business and have now been married 60 years—none of which would've been possible without self-discipline, self-denial, and God's blessing.

Why do you need discipline? Because without it, you give up when things get tough, as they inevitably will. You do what you feel like doing instead of what's necessary. You neglect the things that don't offer immediate gratification—like most things that lead to long-term success.

So if you're pursuing any kind of success, whether in the workplace, your business, marriage, academic studies, managing a household, fitness, the Olympics, or whatever, you need to practise self-discipline and self-denial in your life and in your thinking. They're as essential to success as gas is to running an engine.

"Discipline is the bridge between goals and accomplishment."
– Jim Rohn, entrepreneur, author

"No discipline is enjoyable while it is happening—it's painful! But afterwards there will be a peaceful harvest of right living for those who are trained in this way."
– Hebrews 12:11

29

SETBACKS

Here's an alert for all those in pursuit of success in any area of life, be it career, business, education, or something personal like a relationship or marriage: prepare for setbacks! When setting out to see a dream realized, most of us give little thought to setbacks that may pop up along the way. We may hope that they won't, but this hope is an idle one—as idle as a gardener's hope for a weed-free garden. Setbacks will come. The wise and successful planner anticipates this so as to avoid being blindsided, devastated, and discouraged to the point of quitting when setbacks arise. The wise person also takes advantage of them to try to learn something.

Zig Ziglar, a well-known motivational author and speaker, says this about setbacks: "How many people are completely successful in every department of life? Not one! The most successful people are the ones who learn from their mistakes and setbacks and turn these into opportunities."

Or consider this quote by successful entrepreneur Robert Kiyosaki: "Losers quit when they fail. Winners fail until they succeed." Clearly, for Kiyosaki, setbacks are an inevitable and therefore expected part of succeeding. The secret to dealing with setbacks is to expect these bumps in the road to come along, and when they do—as they will—to accept them without being alarmed or thrown off track. You can deal with them! And you can learn from them. On your success journey you need to be like the baseball player who knows that to hit a home run he must expect to miss some balls. Or like the gardener who knows that to have a perfect garden he'll have to deal with weeds—again and again.

How does one deal with setbacks on one's success journey? This little ditty may help you:

"As you amble on through life, brother, sister, Whatever be your goal,
Keep your eye upon the doughnut And not upon the hole."

That's the key: keep your eye on the goal you started with, pick yourself up, and keep on moving towards it! Determination and persistence will be the tools that help you deal with your setbacks and succeed. Gail Devers, a two-time Olympic champion, advises us to "understand that to achieve anything requires faith and belief in yourself, vision, hard work, determination, and persistence."

Having your eyes open to the possibility of setbacks—being aware, without being afraid—is a prerequisite to succeeding. Taking your setbacks in stride and learning from them qualifies you for success. To be properly prepared is to be a bit like the crew of a cruise ship: while they don't expect disaster, they do carry lifejackets and lifeboats, ready to deal with whatever comes.

"Stay alert and be clearheaded."
- 1 Thessalonians 5:6

30

FAILING IS PART OF SUCCEEDING!

Is it? Well, you be the judge...

- You fell the first time you tried to walk.
- You spoke broken words the first time you tried to talk.
- You almost drowned the first time you tried to swim.
- You fell several times as you tried to learn to skate or ski.
- You missed the ball or dribbled it off the tee as you learned to play golf.
- You fell and scuffed your knees the first time you tried to ride your bike.
- You probably stalled the engine or had a fenderbender when learning to drive.
- You were all thumbs the first time you tried to text a friend.
- You failed some of the tests at school and had to redo them.

"As you continue to journey through life striving to succeed, you'll experience many failures, but don't be alarmed! Failing is part of succeeding. Don't give up, and don't let fear of failure stop you from trying."

– Grandpa/Opa

31

THE YABBUT DISEASE

The yabbut has done its destructive work since the beginning of time. As I amble on through life—now for some 87 years—I marvel at how prevalent and destructive this disease continues to be in the lives of today's promising makers and shakers—just as it was when I enrolled, at age 15, in the U of L (the University of Life, a.k.a. the workplace).

In case you haven't figured it out, yabbut stands for "yeah, BUT!" The "yabbut habit" is a deadly disease that has stopped countless dreams, daring actions, business start-ups, and visions from being realized. It stops promising inventions from ever making it to the drawing board or to completion. In short, it is an all-round achievement and success stopper. The yabbut does to these things what water does to a fire—kills it—or what a nail does to a tire—deflates it. It does to dreams and visions what a stoplight does to traffic: stops it.

The yabbut does its ugly work by raising difficulties as if they were insurmountable. For example, say you plan to start a business and want to use your savings as start-up capital. "Yabbut," says your spouse, "that will mean we can't buy a house!" House-buying being genuinely important, this yabbut ends the discussion and kills the business idea.

You may have heard the yabbut, or said it yourself, in response to a plan. "Yabbut we'd look stupid. Yabbut it'll take too long. Yabbut it's too hard." And there goes another brilliant intent, biting the dust.

The yabbut can also be used in a different way, to justify failure: "Yabbut I just didn't have the time. Yabbut

I forgot. Yabbut I tried, and it didn't work." Or it can be used to rationalize self-indulgence, as when kids are denied something they want and reply, "Yabbut every kid on the street has one." In these cases, the yabbut prevents the person from repenting or learning or changing or growing or exercising self-discipline. Very sad!

Adam and Eve used the yabbut to evade responsibility: "Yabbut Eve made me do it." "Yabbut the serpent tricked me." And when the Israelites—some two million of them—stood at the Jordan River about to take possession of the land promised to them by God, their yabbuts stopped them from realizing that promise: "Yabbut there are giants in the land! Yabbut we'll get killed!" As a result they spent 40 more years in the wilderness, and most never got to enter the Promised Land.

What about your yabbuts? Have they killed some bold ideas you had, or prevented you from breaking through to more daring actions? If you're a Christian, tapped in to God's power, you can change the yabbut to an "and". "And" is open-ended, allowing for further exploration of the obstacles and potential solutions, which can usually be found. It creates room for possibility. "Yabbut that will mean we can't buy a house" becomes "Yes, and if we do that, buying a house will be more difficult." Then, exploring the business opportunity further, you may decide to delay the house purchase, budget more tightly, save for a few more years. You never know what you might come up with to overcome a difficulty!

So, don't let the yabbut disease kill your dreams. Change your yabbut to a "Yes, and" and opportunities will abound.

32

TEAM BUILDING: THE WAY TO SUCCESS

You may be wondering what a Grade 8 dropout could possibly provide by way of valuable team building advice when there are literally hundreds if not thousands of books and articles by experts on the subject. With the foregoing in mind, I'll stay away from telling you what you need to do. Instead I'll just share what I did that developed a productive team over 80 strong, as well as a prosperous business.

As I look back I can see that it wasn't really that complicated. All it took, to start with, was an ambition strong enough to go where opportunity beckons—which included literally moving away from where I lived to the place where an opportunity appeared to be.

The opportunity came in the form of a promising and unique (at that time, in 1963) tire repair franchise, calling on the independent automotive repair trade, car dealerships, and tire shops. Relocation was required, so I packed up the family and away we went. Over the next 40 years I was blessed with success and grew the business to where we became a bona fide wholesale warehouse distributor of automotive parts.

What was the secret? How could a guy with little formal education succeed in a market that was very difficult to penetrate? I don't know all the answers, but I do know some. When we started, we had a unique tire repair that, in terms of quality, remained unduplicated for a couple of years. This gave me a head start. During that period I developed a success strategy that served us well over the remaining 38 years.

Now, here's the team building part: my entire focus was the welfare of our sales staff. I did everything I could to help them earn an excellent income, striving to maximize their—and our customers'—success. I knew that if my sales staff were making money, the company was; if they weren't, we weren't. So 60 percent of my effort was to provide them with product and specials that would help them penetrate the market. We met regularly for mutual support and inspiration and brainstorming.

Nothing is worse for corporate growth than an unhappy salesperson, and to be happy, a salesperson must have a happy customer. Thus the remaining 40 percent of my time, energy, and concentration was spent anticipating and meeting customer needs, discovering what we could do to help our customers prosper in their segment of the market.

So our sales staff became a team with a shared goal, each motivated to pull his or her weight—and since we also shared a goal with our customers, we became a team with them as well. Our inside staff were not left out, either. Well informed and equally well supported, they were fully onside regarding the importance of backing the sales staff.

The result of this simple method was profit and corporate growth. As a Christian I was fully aware that we were also on the receiving end of God's blessings; we didn't do this all by ourselves. Here are the elements that led to a prosperous team:

1. Ambition.
2. A focus on ensuring staff success.
3. Maximizing customer benefits.
4. God's blessing.

"Alone we can do so little; together we can do so much."
– Helen Keller

33

IT'S A HEAD THING

I'm sitting in the eye specialist's chair while he's examining my eyeballs in response to my complaint of having lost my ability to see for about ten minutes earlier that morning. Imagine my surprise when, after the examination, he says, "It's a head thing, Joe; get yourself to Emergency." How could not being able to focus be a head thing and not an eye thing? I was in no rush to get myself to any hospital Emergency department, but go I did, at the urging of my daughter, and discovered that the specialist was right: it was a head thing. I'd had a stroke. This was the first time I realized that I see with my head/brain and not with my eyes.

It's like that with success in your work: it's a head thing. Liking or disliking one's job is something that lives in your mind, and it's your mind that adds to or subtracts from the like or dislike. Feed it enough "dislike" thoughts, and dislike will be produced, resulting in a decline in productivity as well as in the pride and satisfaction that go with a job well done. The end result can't help but have a harmful impact on career advancement.

In other words, career or business success will be elusive, if not outright denied, if you don't have a vision of winning in your head; a vision of winning had better be there before you put a shovel in the ground or invest your first nickel. That's because your thinking will determine your action and how much effort you're prepared to put forth in pursuing your goal.

I'm not promoting positive thinking as the end-all and be-all. When I say that success is a head thing, I also mean that you need to use your head and carefully consider the pros and cons of a venture, not letting either overly optimistic thinking carry you away nor unduly negative thoughts stop you from stepping out of the boat. Rather, whatever the venture, engage in it with sober thought and after prayer for insight and wisdom. Then be realistic about the difficulties you're likely to face and how you will overcome them.

Let's get back to liking or disliking one's job. What role does the head play in that? Dislike has to be fed to live, just as a fire has to be fed to burn. So be honest and realistic about your work situation, but don't give those dislike thoughts so much oxygen! Give some good will a chance to come to the fore. Think about the positives of your work, and about how your job satisfaction will be improved by giving it full-on effort. Think about specific things you can do better in your job, and then let that guide your actions.

Imagine Joseph sold by his brothers into slavery: I'm betting he didn't like where he was or the job he was handed. But he dug into it with all of his might and power, and was consequently promoted to the running of Potiphar's business empire and eventually the entire land of Egypt. He kept himself from being bogged down by negative thoughts, and fed his mind instead with visions of what could happen if he gave everything he had to the tasks assigned to him, knowing that God was with him. You can do the same. Be one who thinks clearly, sees possibilities in every situation, and gives your all to whatever job comes your way!

"Those who work hard will prosper."
– Proverbs 23:4

34

STANDARDS

Hey, Success Pursuer, here are a few questions for you:

1. What standards for work and behaviour do you set for yourself when it comes to honesty, ethics, work, punctuality, dependability, productivity, etc.?
2. Are these standards high enough?
3. Do you live these standards, or are you one who says, "Do as I say, don't do as I do."?
4. Are your expectations of yourself the same as your expectations of others?
5. If your family and the folk in your workplace adopted your actual lived standards and followed your example in all the abovementioned areas, what kind of a family life would you have? Would it be a happy one? And would your workplace be a happy and productive place?

If, in answer to the last question, you realize that following your example in your family or workplace would not result in the happiness and productivity you yourself are seeking, then change is in order—assuming you're serious about that quest.

I have found that expecting little from yourself produces little for yourself, and that expecting more from others than you do from yourself is an equally dead-end street. In other words, the success you are pursuing will continue to elude you, and you will fail in your career, business, workplace, marriage, and faith-walk with the Lord, unless you set high standards for yourself—standards you are determined to meet in spite of setbacks and difficulties.

How do you know whether your standards are the right ones? That's easy; it's where the fifth question above comes in. Just ask yourself: If my family and co-workers adopted my standards and poured the same degree of effort and the same kind of attitudes into their goals that I pour into mine, would their happiness and prosperity be enhanced? If the answer to this is a resounding YES, then your standards are worth keeping. Continue to strive to meet them. If the answer is NO, then you need to raise your standards, or start seriously aiming for them if you haven't been doing so. When you do, you'll find yourself well on the way to God-honouring success in any endeavour you pour your talents and energy into.

Remember: your actions and your words should always agree. The standard you profess should be the standard you actually strive to meet each day. Let your example be worthy of following. Your actions will prove you're committed to living a new life.

"Raise your standards and aim for greatness."
– Author Unknown

"The quality of a leader is reflected in the standards they set for themselves."
– Roy Kroc (builder of the McDonalds empire)

"Refuse to lower your standards to accommodate those who refuse to raise theirs."
– Mandy Hale (Author)

"The Lord detests double standards of every kind."
– Proverbs 20:10

35

STANDING OUT

Who among us wouldn't like to stand out in our workplace as a capable, trustworthy, conscientious worker? And when it comes to one's business, what's nicer and more profitable than to stand out in the marketplace as a supplier of quality products, always providing outstanding customer care and delivering on promises?

Everybody wants to stand out. But how can this desirable and vital status be attained? Most corporations in pursuit of growth and market share will spend lot of money to stand out in the marketplace and in the minds of potential customers—mostly, though not exclusively, through advertising, which eats up millions and millions of dollars. If you advertise enough, you will stand out in people's minds even if your product and service are mediocre.

But what about standing out personally, at work or wherever God has placed us? How can we be recognized as unique and valuable, other than by our performance? We can't advertise; that comes across as blowing our own horn, being conceited, or as buttering up the boss.

But there is a kind of attention-getting communication that is altogether honourable, and mostly overlooked. And it's easy! When I tell you what it is, you'll probably say, "Of course! Why didn't I think of that?" It consists of just two words that cost nothing but produce amazing results in terms of making you stand out—but only when handwritten and mailed. They are: "Thank you!" These are the words that will help your career, grow your business, strengthen relationships, build character, and establish you as a caring person—in the eyes of the God who created you. Gratitude is not only attractive, but right; we are to be thankful people, not only to God but to others. Remember, though: your thank-you, to stand out, must be handwritten and mailed to the person you genuinely want to thank for something of value they did for you. Simple, eh?

Let's take a look at what will happen if you do what I'm suggesting here. Say you've made a sales presentation that produced a buy. You get home and write a postcard, mail it to the buyer, and all it says is: "Thank you, Joe, for seeing me and giving me an order. It's much appreciated." When the buyer gets this handwritten thank-you either at his home or work, I guarantee he or she will remember you! You'll stand out! Or suppose a colleague helped you catch up with your heavy workload. You write and mail a card to her that says, "Thank you, Alice, for helping me yesterday. I'm grateful." You will be remembered!

You see, gratitude is scarcer than it ought to be; people are pleasantly surprised by it. Also, people don't get much handwritten personal mail these days, if any; writing and mailing a message requires an unusual, if small, investment of time and effort. So when people are thanked with a handwritten, snail-mailed note, they feel valued—and they in turn appreciate and remember the one who has honoured them in this way. But take note, a thank-you must not be used to manipulate or to angle for favours or other personal gain. For it to produce blessing, your thank-you has to be a sincere expression of gratitude. That's how you stand out!

"At midnight I rise to give you thanks."
– Psalm 19:62

36

100 PERCENT RESPONSIBLE

Let me introduce you to the one hundred percenters: the folk who, when they see a situation that is not as it should be, take steps to correct it. Yes, there are folk like that! Maybe you are among this winning group yourself: you see something that needs doing, and you do it. Most winners have this I-hold-myself-one-hundred-percent-responsible attitude.

In the vocabulary of the one hundred percenters, the words "that's not my job" don't exist. When they walk into the office and see an overflowing wastebasket, they empty it, even though it's not their job. When they see a colleague's desk overflowing with work, they say, "Can I give you a hand?" instead of pretending they don't see the person struggling. A one hundred percenter on the factory or warehouse floor has the same "How can I help?" and "Let me pitch in" attitude.

These one hundred percenters are sometimes accused of being a "company man" or "company woman", to which I say, "But of course they are!" What this means is that when they see something that's detrimental to corporate welfare—and thus to the welfare of their fellow workers or employees—they automatically take responsibility to see that the situation is corrected, as any responsible person should. This behaviour and attitude are essential to success in any field, whether in producing a happy marital relationship or securing business and career advancement. If you don't correct the things you see that aren't as they ought to be, or for improving what needs to be improved, on your own initiative, how can you move towards success at all? You will be one of the "that's not my job" crowd. This crowd does nothing to produce success—for themselves or for the enterprise they're part of, whatever it is. Their attitude shoots everybody in the foot, including themselves!

If it's your responsibility to contribute to the success of the enterprise you're part of, it's also true that your own self-advancement is one hundred percent your responsibility, one hundred percent of the time. Of course, as a Christian you will be, and need to be, praying for success. However, over my 87 years of life—70 of them in the workplace, and 40 of those as an employer—I have seen many prayers unanswered and success denied because the person praying had an "I'll leave it to God" attitude when God was saying, "Do something I can bless! Quit this waiting, get up off your knees, and start taking responsibility for the things you can and need to do!"

You see, as human beings we're given the privilege and res-ponsibility of partnering with God. So if it's a promotion you're seeking, take some evening courses and upgrade yourself. If it's a job, start sending out résumés and knockng on doors. These are actions God can bless. We need God's blessing to be successful in whatever God-honouring endeavour we want to be successful in. However, as the old saying goes, "Pray and work." The successful person takes 100% responsibility to do their part so God can do his.

You will eat the fruit of your labour; blessings and prosperity will be yours. - Psalm 128:2

May the favour of the Lord our God rest on us; establish the work of our hands. - Psalm 90:17

37
JOB SATISFACTION

The title says it all, doesn't it? Job satisfaction is something all of us in the workplace, wherever and whatever that may be, would like to experience every day.

But for many of us that's just not happening. And when we don't have job satisfaction, many of us start thinking that to find it we have to change jobs. Then when we succeed in finding a new job, we are chagrined to discover that job satisfaction is not to be had there either! So, once again we make another job search, in pursuit of the ideal job. It has to be there somewhere!

The unfortunate thing is that this search will end in failure no matter how many times we embark on it. Why is that? Well, it's because we're ignoring one of the laws that govern success. The law in question is the Law of Input. It is the law that says "Input determines output"—meaning that you only get out of something what you put in. Nowhere is this truer than when it comes to job satisfaction.

Quite simply, to experience job satisfaction you've got to give the job your all—no matter what that job is, and even if you're not keen on it. If you start giving it your whole-hearted effort, you'll be amazed at what happens. The job in question could be as simple as sweeping a warehouse floor. It may have received only a fraction of your effort and your heart, and thus was incapable of producing the personal pride and satisfaction that come from a job well done. The only thing that produces job satisfaction is striving to excel at whatever you're asked to do; it's one hundred percent effort, one hundred percent of the time! In other words, it doesn't come from the outside at all; it comes from the inside, and is directly proportional to what you put in. That, in turn, means that this wonderful feeling is available in full measure to the sweeper or washroom cleaner, just as it is to the highest official in the corporate arena, provided they give it their all.

Do that, and job satisfaction is guaranteed. It is God's blessing on a job well done. He simply can't bless half-hearted effort, so give it your all and experience job satisfaction.

> *"Better a little which is well done*
> *than a great deal done imperfectly."*
> – Plato

"The reward of a thing well done is having done it."
– Ralph Waldo Emerson (philosopher, poet, author, essayist)

38
DUTY AT WORK

Though I've already written a blog called "The Beauty of Duty", I'm writing this one exclusively focused on the workplace and one's career or business.

The word "duty", the rare time it's heard today, is mostly inadequately understood, and hardly ever applied to self. Give yourself 20 seconds to name at least five things you would accept as your duty; then ask yourself whether, or how often, you have ever thought of these in terms of your duty. I dare say that seeing them as duty doesn't feature largely in your thinking. But there's no doubt that a clear understanding and acceptance of duty is absolutely vital to your success at work, in your career or business.

Think of the soldiers in an army: the call to duty must be obeyed at all costs and without question. If they ignore or refuse to do their duty, the army loses the battle, and ultimately the war. Like soldiers, we have battles to fight on the way to success, and we will not be victorious unless we recognize and carry out our duty. Like soldiers, we are part of something bigger than ourselves, a shared enterprise that claims our wholehearted effort. And as with the soldier, doing our duty involves sacrifice on our part, and a willingness to submit to the daily demands of a job whether we feel like it or not.

As workers, we all have a duty to do our jobs as well as we possibly can at all times. All workers—from those making deliveries or cleaning the washrooms to those engaged in administrative work or management, right up to the president or owner of a corporation—

have a duty to give their all to their work, all of the time, not just when they feel like it. We owe this to ourselves, our families, our co-workers, our clients, and ultimately to God, who has placed us where we are and has given us our work.

Don't get me wrong; without doubt, the best and most satisfying work is done when a sense of duty is combined with passion for what you're doing. But in every job, there are long stretches, or unavoidable aspects of the work, where we just don't feel like it—when the only thing that compels us to give the necessary wholehearted effort is understanding and accepting it as our duty. Duty entertains no reasons or excuses; more pressing even than responsibility, duty insists on being carried out no matter what. When all other motivating factors fail, duty remains a non-negotiable claim on us. It is something we owe, the minimum that can be expected of us.

I've learned by experience that the career and business growth of a person who recognizes and accepts duty will surpass that of those who only think of responsibility (although a responsible attitude is desirable). I was fortunate to have both kinds in my company, and the duty-takers were the ones on whom I could rely one hundred percent, one hundred percent of the time. They're the kind of person you want to have on the other oar when asked to cross the ocean in a rowboat. They're the sort that build careers and companies—the kind of soldiers who make winning armies. May you be among this group.

"We are unworthy servants; we have only done our duty."
– Luke 17:10

39

THE FIXER

As we amble through life, there are inevitably things that break down and need fixing. Most of us accept breakdowns, though unwelcome, as more or less normal when it comes to mechanical things such as cars, dishwashers, computers and so on. And we can call on a whole group of professional technicians to do the fixing—including physicians, where our health is concerned.

However, there's another type of breakdown where we can't just hand the problem off to a professional. Even if a professional is available and can be of some help, the onus of fixing falls squarely on oneself. I'm referring to breakdowns of a personal nature, such as the kind that happen in our workplaces. Conflict with colleagues can be the cause of unbearable workplace stress, poisoning the atmosphere to such an extent that in extreme cases one chooses to resign—which can be a real career setback—rather than fix the problem. Or we have marital breakdowns, many of which don't get fixed and end painfully in divorce. And in the corporate world, whole businesses break down and go under unless their problems are fixed.

The "Fixer" in each of these breakdowns is none other than the very one involved in the breakdown. If you're involved, YOU are the fixer. Yes, you read that right—you!

"But," you say, "I'm not a fixer, was never taught the skill." That's okay, and that's why I'm writing this brief blog. So, what does it take to fix a breakdown of this kind?

1. Pray for wisdom, and trust that it will be given.
2. Reflect on the situation and identify the problem.
3. Have a genuine desire to see it fixed.
4. Accept responsibility for fixing it; don't wait for someone else to do it.
5. Have a clear mind-picture of what the situation will look like once fixed.
6. Write down what needs to happen to see it fixed.
7. Proceed to implement number 6, trusting God to bless your action.

Note that, whether it's a problem at one's workplace or a marriage in difficulty, the cure always includes taking personal responsibility to see the problem solved and not waiting for someone else to take needed action. Let me share a couple of personal examples.

I worked as a coffee truck driver for a very successful company. There were 120 of us when the Teamsters Union approached, wanting us to join their union. Since we were doing great without them, we resisted. When the union responded by blocking us from many construction sites and clients we were serving, we driver-salespeople, and the company we represented, were worried. A possible strike loomed. What to do? I was "only" an employee, but I took personal responsibility and came up with a solution: form our own in-house association and register it as a legal entity. Presto! The Teamsters left us alone and we preserved our excellent relationship with our employer as well as our well-paying jobs. God blessed my action.

Here's another example: my marriage was in jeopardy. I had been waiting for many years for my wife to change, but that hadn't happened, and the harmony of our home was broken. Having read God's word, where it says, "Do to others as you would have others do to you," and "You will reap what you sow," I thought I'd better start doing what it said and believe that different sowing—an attitude of loving concern, open discussion of what troubled me, kindness instead of resentment, and a willingness to change my own behaviour—would lead to different reaping. I trusted that God would bless my changed attitude, and that I would reap the benefit in my marriage. Sure enough, it worked!

The lesson? Pray for wisdom, believe, reflect, take responsibility, and act—realizing that the action required may be a change in your own attitudes and behaviour. Do this in your marriage as well as in your workplace, and you'll see things that are broken move towards being fixed.

"Do unto others as you would like them to do to you."
– Jesus (Luke 6:31)

40

YOUR THIRD EYE

Like most other people, you are likely unaware that you have a third eye; but you do. And this eye is often the reason your promising ideas never get a chance to prove their worth. The third eye can be death to a great idea.

That's because this eye tends to see trouble and difficulty ahead if your idea were to be implemented. It sees mountains where there are molehills, magnifying small difficulties so they show up on the screen of your mind as big problems that should be avoided at all costs.

Where is this third eye? It's in your mind. It is one of Satan's most effective tools to kill bold ideas and paralyze daring action. It's not that your mind's eye is by nature bad, of course; you need to be able to foresee difficulty so you can address it. I get to this below. But this third eye is easily hijacked by Satan, or even by your own insecurity, to magnify the negative like a shadow thrown on the wall by a flame. If not carefully monitored and controlled, your third eye will destroy your confidence. Soon this becomes a habit, and you shrivel up inside. No more big ideas.

Now, like I said, your mind's eye is not a bad thing. This third eye is also the one that envisions the wonderful result of implementing your bold idea. That vision is what prompted you to consider acting on the idea in the first place. The third eye is also the one that works to imagine solutions to problems. So you don't want to just shut it off. Denial is not the answer. So what is?

The answer is to acknowledge the negative and get it out of your mind where it keeps clouding the positive.

One of the best ways to do this is to write it down. That's right: transfer your third eye's negative input to paper, a whiteboard, or whatever, so that the third eye is freed up to see the positive that was there all along, and to come up with solutions to problems. Fully recognizing and acknowledging the negative and giving it a form in the material world clears it out of your third eye. It's a sort of mind rinse.

The screen of your mind can only display one issue at a time. If it's monopolized by the negative, the positive part of your imagination gets no screen time and can't do its wonderful problem-solving work. The mind rinse frees you to develop the idea so you can entertain a positive, winning vision instead of the negative, losing one.

So many people let the negative and the positive endlessly bounce back and forth in their minds, till they lose sleep, grow weary, and stress out. They never arrive at a decision, and end up dropping the whole idea. If that's you, it's very sad. Any of these ideas may have been God's call on your life, and Satan has hijacked your mind's eye to squash it, all while persuading you that you're just being a careful realist.

The Bible says, "You can't heal a wound you deny you have." The answer is not to ignore the negative input of your third eye, but to let it work on solving problems by getting them off your mental screen and down on paper. You can do this with God's help. Acknowledge to him that your screen is full of negative images, write them down, and ask him for the creativity to imagine solutions.

"With God we will gain the victory."
– Psalm 60:12

41

THE IDEAL

Success demands that there be an ideal in your vision and dreams, an ideal that you are striving to realize. And though you may never fully achieve this idyllic state, be it in your job, business, marriage, or whatever, even partial success demands that you continue pursuing your ideal anyway. Having a very clear vision of this ideal will guide your efforts and also provide the stimulation for you to persist and stay the course in spite of difficulties or roadblocks.

But when you give up the chase and begin lowering your standards, it's a sure thing that your reduced effort will never produce anything like the desired result that seemed achievable at first. When you allow yourself to start thinking "It'll never happen," failure becomes the likely outcome. This is true whether you're pursuing a university diploma, a graduate degree, a loving marital relationship, a better job, a more profitable business, a fitter body, or any other goal. You need to have a vision of your ideal and you need to keep that vision before you at all times.

Anne Frank writes, "Everyone has inside of him or her a piece of good news. The good news is that you don't know how great you can be! How much you can love! What you can accomplish! And what your potential is."

In order to be released, this potential Anne is talking about requires that your ideal be much alive in your heart and mind, and that you keep cultivating the desire to see it become a reality. I am convinced that what kept Edison going through defeat after defeat in his pursuit to develop the light bulb was the vision of the ideal in his mind's eye: a light-giving unit so superior to candles or oil lamps in the lighting of our homes. His ideal is now an everyday piece of household equipment.

Carl Schurz, author and film director, says, "Ideals are like stars: you will not succeed in touching them with your hands, but like the seafaring man on the desert of waters, you choose them as your guides, and following them you reach your destiny."

A clear vision and understanding of the ideal you are pursuing in any area of your life will keep you motivated and working towards it. In the process you'll likely experience some defeats and setbacks, just like Edison; but you'll also experience many victories, and you'll be living a rewarding and vibrant life.

Marriage is a good example of this. A keen awareness of the ideal you have not yet achieved with your spouse, and a strong desire to see it realized, will cause you to work at making it so. This kind of desire and effort will have the blessing of the Lord and may well produce a sixty-year marriage. I know, for that's what happened in my case.

The ideal: we may not fully achieve it in our jobs, marriages, or other areas of life, but don't let that stop you from pursuing it. That pursuit is an essential component of ultimate success. And as you proceed along these paths, be sure you stay plugged in to God-power.

"I will guide you along the best pathway for your life.
I will advise you and watch over you."
– Psalm 32:8

42

ENCOURAGE

I recently read something written by Mart DeHaan (a noted writer and author) that is so true, and so vital to personal as well as corporate success, that I'm going to quote it here:

> *"In the workplace, words of encouragement matter. How employees talk to one another has a bearing on customer satisfaction, company profits, and co-worker appreciation. Studies show that members of the most effective workgroups give one another six times more affirmation than disapproval, disagreement, or sarcasm. Least productive teams tend to use almost three negative comments for every helpful word."*

Wow. Those are surprising statistics! They compel each of us to ask ourselves, about our presence at work: Am I an encourager or a critic? Do I build people up or tear them down? Am I affirming or am I disapproving? Am I one who tries to contribute to a pleasant work environment, or do I contribute to a rotten atmosphere? Do I see customers as the most important part of our business, or do I see them as an interruption, a pain in the neck with all their demands? And here's the final question: Based on the above, am I a part of the most effective work group, or do I belong to the least productive one?

If it's the latter, it's time you made up your mind to bring about positive change at work—first in your thinking, and then in your behaviour. Count yourself out of the down-at-the-mouth, unhappy group, and join the cheerful, going-places gang. Compliment people; thank them. Make encouraging, affirming comments. Be sincere and helpful. Smile at people; make them laugh sometimes (but not at anyone else's expense). If criticism is necessary, make sure it's constructive and gentle, and not mere faultfinding. And respond courteously, with an open mind, when receiving criticism yourself.

By doing these things you'll raise the effectiveness quotient of your workplace, as well as its general tone. Then you—and your colleagues—will soon be able to say, "Thank God for Monday morning too," instead of only looking forward to Friday and the weekend.

This change in attitude and behaviour, like any other one that matters, won't be easy; but you can do it if you stick to it and seek God's help.

> *"There's no thrill in easy sailing,*
> *When the sky is clear and blue;*
> *There's no joy in merely doing*
> *Things which anyone can do.*
> *But there is some satisfaction*
> *That is mighty sweet to take,*
> *When you've reached a destination*
> *That you thought you couldn't make."*
> – Author Unknown

"So encourage each other and build each other up."
– 1 Thessalonians 5:11

43

KEEP THE POWER ON

What does an airplane have in common with success in a person's life? For both, it takes a lot of power and effort to get to the desired level; and to stay there, both have to keep the power on. And what's the difference between a pilot flying a 747 that has reached its 30,000 ft. flying level and a person who has achieved a measure of success—such as a high school diploma, university degree, workplace promotion, or flourishing business?

The difference is that whereas the pilot always keeps the power on, though he may turn it down a bit, the successful person often turns the power off! After all, they've arrived, and can now take it easy, right? This translates into no more study or reading, no fresh input, no tackling new challenges, and no ongoing effort. And that all too often leads to being overtaken by co-workers in one's workplace, losing ground to competitors in the business world, stagnation in self-development, or the gradual erosion of one's skills and knowledge. In other words, you end up being left behind careerwise, or going broke businesswise.

Two examples in the retail world are Eaton's and Sears. Both used to be household words; now they're defunct. Or consider Blackberry, the giant in the electronics field that pretty well had the phone market sewn up: management thought they had arrived, and then they lost focus. They started purchasing hockey teams and pursuing other sidelines, and their competitors caught up, passed them, and brought them close to bankruptcy. There are many companies, big and small, and many individuals, who similarly took the power off and ended up biting the dust.

I trust you now see the similarity between success in a person's life and the 747 flying at 30,000 ft.

Dear successful one, regardless of where you are in your career, profession, marriage, business, or spiritual life, the minute you quit making a whole-hearted effort you will start losing height. And if you're not careful to refuel with renewed energy, drive, focus, and enthusiasm, and keep the power on, you'll end up like a plane whose pilot takes the power off: crashed. A has-been.

Many marriages are victim to this "powering down". The courting produced the marriage, and once we have arrived at the altar and exchanged vows, so many of us drop the courting attitude and behaviour that led to the union, naively expecting to continue to fly high. Well, you know the statistics on that; maybe you're one of them. If you are, then the next time (if there is a next time for you), you will be wiser and know enough to keep the power on.

Any successful endeavour that is not constantly fed and tended will wither like a neglected plant. Don't let that happen to you! And if it did once, don't let it happen the second time.

"And let us run with endurance the race God has set before us."
— Hebrews 12:1

44

STOP AND REFLECT

While in hot pursuit of career or business success, a person doesn't often stop and reflect. In fact, you may wonder, why stop at all when things are going well? That is, if they are going well for you. But whether they are or not, stopping and reflecting periodically, while pursuing success in whatever worthy cause or objective you have set for yourself, is strongly recommended. It's like the practice of a master carpenter, busy working on a job, who pauses to measure twice so that he or she only saws once; the extra measuring step avoids a lot of wrong cuts and wasted material. Or think of a wise builder who takes time to consult the blueprints on a regular basis to make sure that everything going up on the site is as drawn and planned. This must be done repeatedly if the 50 storeys being built are to stand securely.

This stopping and checking is really an essential part in the building of anything. When it comes to your career or business, it involves placing your fully written sheet of goals and objectives—you'd better have one—on your desk in front of you, and going over it carefully to see whether you're still on target and have reached your objectives by the timelines you had set. If not, then think of what remedial steps you need to take to get back on target. Of course, as part of your reflection, you should also rethink your original goals and objectives and re-confirm that they are still what you want to see realized. If you find this not to be the case, then this is the time for a new goal sheet to be written.

For example, you may have set your sights on becoming a surgeon, but as you study to achieve this, you conclude that flesh-cutting is really not your cup of tea. Or a hockey career may be the star you are reaching for, but as you become involved, your desire may wane. This will become clear as you stop and reflect. If so, it's wise to change course. Likewise, if you're starting a business, review your corporate goal sheet regularly, with its market penetration objectives and deadlines. Are you on target in these? If not, what needs to change?

Failure to stop and reflect is liable to result in unpleasant and costly surprises that could have been avoided. In sports, I'm told, successful managers review every game—those lost, to see what contributed to the loss and should be avoided in future, and those won, to see what could have been done even better and what should be repeated.

Most of us on a winning curve are loath to look at what we could or should have done better or check to see if there are market threats we need to be guard against. Regular stops for in-depth reflection prevent setbacks and produce ongoing prosperity. Had Blackberry— leader in the industry at the time—engaged in some reflecton, I doubt they'd have been relegated to the sidelines as they were.

"Follow effective action with quiet reflection. From the quiet reflection will come even more effective action."
– Peter Drucker (Management consultant)

"But you did not consider these things or reflect on what might happen."
– Isaiah 47:7

45

LIFE'S INSTRUCTIONS

When, at the urging of my eldest daughter, I started writing my memoirs and spent a lot of time looking back on the events of my life, I began to see how so much of life is actually ongoing instruction. We don't notice this when we're in the midst of events; what should be an instruction to make me wiser is seen then only as a pain in the neck. Our failure to recognize these often-unpleasant happenings as instructions, when they occur, is the reason we have to re-learn the same lessons.

Reflecting on this in my own life, I wondered, Why is this so? Why did I make the same mistakes again and again? I believe I now have the answer, and in sharing this with you I hope that wisdom will come much earlier in your life than it did in mine.

It was during one of my recent morning devotions that I read, "Whoever gives heed to instruction prospers, and blessed is the one who trusts in the Lord" (Proverbs 16:20). The first part of the verse, about heeding instruction, was an eye-opener. I realized, looking back, that I had never perceived the many less-than-pleasant happenings in my life as instructions that could have helped me become wiser if I'd heeded and followed them.

We should learn from every happening in life, good or bad. What a simple idea that is! Imagine how much wiser I would have been had I known this sooner! So how can we develop that habit? I know how: by remembering just five words (one "handful") we need to ask after every notable experience. If you discipline yourself to say these five words every time you experience something significant—good or bad—and trust the Lord to guide your thinking as you do so, you'll develop the wisdom that leads to a prosperous, happy, and fulfilled life. The five words are: What's the instruction in this?

Here are some examples. You're late for dinner and your wife's angry because dinner's cold. You ask yourself: What's the instruction in this? The answer's obvious: be considerate and phone next time! Or say you're generally rushed in the morning and have to speed in order to get to work on time; you get your second speeding ticket in a month. What's the instruction in this? Get out of bed earlier so you won't be so rushed! Note that I say instruction rather than lesson. That's because a lesson can be mere information, a principle, a concept; but an instruction calls for action. Life's instructions call us to do something. They call us to change our behaviour, or, in the case of a good experience, to continue it—as when, out of the blue, you come home with a bouquet of flowers for your wife. Oh happy, happy wife, and a pleasant atmosphere all evening! You ask: What's the instruction in this? Do this more often, as it's a blessed thing to do and brings happiness.

So remember: after all happenings, hold up your hand, look at your five fingers, and ask: What's the instruction in this?

> *"Whoever gives heed to instruction prospers, and blessed is the one who trusts in the Lord."*
> – Proverbs 16:20

46

CONFLICT IN THE WORKPLACE

Very few people, other than perhaps the most belligerent among us, welcome conflict. Most people don't like to clash with co-workers, family members, or anyone else, and some of us will even go to great lengths to avoid any and all relational friction.

Often, people seek to avoid conflict by hearing no evil, seeing no evil, and speaking no evil. At least speaking no evil doesn't actively contribute to conflict; but refusing to hear or see evil is useless in avoiding or resolving conflict. Such a strategy is like closing your eyes to weeds in your garden: it's not only foolish, but counterproductive, as it'll allow the weeds to take over. Or think of a wound that is left untreated: it has a good chance of becoming infected, or even gangrenous. Similarly, unaddressed conflict will poison relationships. Just like the weeds in the garden, or the infection in the wound, it will lead to ever-expanding workplace discord, and may even prevent corporate expansion and growth by killing the team spirit that all healthy corporations need in order to bring about success.

So, how should one deal with conflict in general, and in the workplace in particular?

The first step is to admit there is a conflict. Go to the person or people involved, identify the core issue, and have a conversation that is respectful, positive, and befitting your role as either a colleague or a superior. Obviously, if you are speaking to a peer, your manner will be different from that of someone in authority. In either case, it's important to listen as much as you speak.

Here's a case history. It was our custom to have

one of our staff replace our receptionist during lunch breaks. This involved physically sitting in the reception cubicle. One day, noticing the replacement staffer sitting some distance from the desk instead of behind it, I asked why. I was informed that our receptionist had a hygiene problem, and the lingering odour made her replacements nauseous. Apparently this had been going on for some time and had already triggered conflict between reception and replacements; the problem had produced a lot of bad feelings all around, with co-workers taking sides. Since no one was willing to tackle the issue, it fell to me as CEO to do so. I did, though I felt uncomfortable. The problem was faced, dealt with, and resolved.

In another case, a long-time, very valuable employee had begun to be abusive in her behaviour and language. I was informed, but did not want to deal with it because of her long-time service and because several of her family members were also employed by my firm. So I ignored the conflict, hoping it would go away. As a consequence of my foolish, cowardly, and irresponsible inaction, our office atmosphere was poisoned! We were no longer a happy workplace. The problem only ended when the culprit finally quit, after a lot of damage had been done. My failure to address the conflict was inexcusable and a dereliction of my duty as CEO and owner.

But you don't have to be a CEO or manager to address conflict in your workplace. Especially as a Christian, you can often be a peacemaker. If you see that people are at odds, that it's affecting their work and potentially the spirit of the workplace, and if you have any personal currency with those involved, you can speak to them in a collegial manner. I know a retail worker who saw a conflict quickly escalating between two of her colleagues, until neither would speak to the other. Not only did this keep them from necessary collaboration, but they enlisted the sympathies of other colleagues and created tension in the general atmosphere, which had previously been open and friendly. The one who observed this called each of her colleagues aside separately and discreetly, listened first, and then spoke as a friend and peer about how they could respond differently. It took several days for the two to reach the point where they could sit down and resolve the conflict, but they did, and went on to work well together.

Remember: identify the conflict, put it on the table, and deal with it in a respectful, understanding way. Most problems can be solved, and all need to be faced and dealt with to avoid festering.

> *"In conflict-solving be fair and generous."*
> – Lao Tzu (ancient Chinese philosopher)

> *"A hot-tempered person stirs up conflict,*
> *but the one who is patient calms a quarrel."*
> – Proverbs 15:18

47

YOUR GOODWILL ACCOUNT

We all know about bank accounts, and how life has a way of becoming stressful if they're not in good shape. And we all know about charge accounts, which includes credit cards; most of us have more than one of those, and most of us also know we'd better not overload them if we want to live tranquil lives. People with heavy credit card debt are inevitably plagued with financial insecurity and anxiety. It's my hope you are not in this group.

Credit cards and charge accounts deal with money, of course, and are mostly held by banks or businesses. However, there's another type of account that we all have, whether we know it or not. It's the goodwill account, and deposits made into it are not financial. What's so unique about this account is that we all have one we hold ourselves, as well as many others held for us by our friends, family members, co-workers, business associates, neighbours, and any other people with whom we rub shoulders. These goodwill accounts have one thing in common with our bank accounts: you can draw out only what you've deposited, or you'll run into difficulties. There are, unfortunately, no overdraft privileges here.

What does this goodwill account look like, and why is it held for you by other people? Valid question. Your goodwill deposits are all the kindnesses you've done for someone, all the help you've offered or given them, the promises you've made and kept, the patience or forgiveness you've shown—even the gratitude you've expressed when you were on the receiving end yourself.

All these kind actions, and others of the same nature, are deposits in the goodwill account you have with that person. When you in turn need help from them, you can draw on the goodwill you've built up in the relationship; it's a very valuable asset!

In the workplace, this goodwill account is vital for career and business growth. For example, say you've just helped your colleague solve a problem, or maybe even just brought her a coffee without being asked. This is a deposit in your goodwill account, the one they are holding with your name on it. It helps to make them well-disposed towards you; that's what goodwill means. You can look forward to that colleague's help or support when you need it, or their simple good wishes and friendly acknowledgment when you don't. They in turn are either building a goodwill account with you, or trying to make withdrawals when there's nothing there to withdraw. An overdraft on a goodwill account produces nothing but resentment and ill will, which bodes no good for either party in the relationship.

In a business, goodwill deposits are made with suppliers, for example, by paying bills on time, dealing fairly, expressing gratitude for what they contribute to your business, and not abusing the supplier relationship with unreasonable demands. Goodwill deposits are made with clients or customers by delivering quality products or services in a timely fashion for a fair price, offering helpful information, and going the extra mile to provide what they need or to honour your guarantee.

In all our relationships we are either making goodwill deposits or making withdrawals. Our relationships run so much more smoothly when our goodwill accounts are kept topped up with regular deposits. But take note! It doesn't take much by way of withdrawals to empty an account, so you need to be careful. Keep your withdrawals as few and as modest as you can. You may want to check the current bottom line in your goodwill account with your boss, colleagues, or employees, or with your spouse. Do you have a healthy balance in there, or are you in danger of being overdrawn?

Jesus said, "As you give, so shall you receive." This truth applies here as it does everywhere else. Be someone who makes plenty of goodwill deposits to those in your sphere of influence, and you will reap much blessing.

48

ESSENTIALS

An essential ingredient to a lasting marriage is commitment; to a well-built house it's a solid foundation; and to a healthy body it's proper hygiene, a balanced diet, and exercise. I don't think any of you have a problem in recognizing all these as essentials.

What's essential to success? Most of us, if not all, are in pursuit of success of some sort, whether it's a high school diploma, a college or university degree, the establishment or growth of a business, the advancement of a career, or even the simple—but often difficult—task of balancing a budget.

Not knowing the essential ingredient makes it well-nigh impossible to achieve success. You'd be like a builder not knowing about the need for a solid foundation, or a person seeking to build a lasting marriage without knowing the essential ingredient of commitment, imagining that all it takes is a little romance. Not knowing in these cases leads to not doing, with failure as the result.

So what's the ingredient essential to success? It's discipline!!! Not discipline imposed from the outside, but self-discipline. It's the ability to deny yourself—to keep your nose to the grindstone when others are having fun, stay the course when the going gets tough, resist self-indulgence so you can use your money, energy, and time in pursuit of your goal, keep the promises you made to yourself and others, and refuse to give up until the goal's been reached. Difficult? Yes, it is, but to achieve the success you're pursuing, that's what has to be done. And now that you know the not-so-secret ingredient, I trust you'll put it into practice.

Here are a few quotes from people who've walked the discip-line road:

"We all have dreams. But in order to make dreams come into reality, it takes an awful lot of determination, dedication, self-discipline, and effort."
– Jesse Owens, Olympic athlete

"With faith, self-discipline, and selfless devotion to duty, there is nothing worthwhile that you cannot achieve."
– Muhammad Ali Jinnah, lawyer, politician, and first Governor-General of Pakistan

"Their purpose is to teach people to live disciplined and successful lives, to help them do what is right, just, and fair."
– Proverbs 1:3

"To learn, you must love discipline."
– Proverbs 12:1

49

MAINTENANCE

When you buy or lease a new car, it comes with a recommended maintenance plan. This document lists items that the manufacturer suggests you get checked at certain mileage intervals in order to keep the car in sound running condition. Ignore the advice, and the consequences are always unpleasant and mostly expensive. A similar principle applies to our bodies: no doubt most of us wash daily, have a physical now and then, walk or exercise, and watch what we eat. This is all wise and necessary if we want to reach old age.

The fact is, maintenance is needed at work, too; there are things that must be checked regularly if work is to go well. Funnily enough, though, when it comes to the workplace, few of us follow any maintenance schedule—even though we spend a third of our lives there. What if we as business owners, supervisors, employees, homemakers, contractors, or students—whatever our work is—were to voluntarily ask for a performance evaluation every six months or year? Things like productivity, carefulness, teamwork, initiative, attitude, management style, and relationships with others in the workplace would all be checked. And what if, during this exercise, we were to ask for suggestions as to how we could improve, so we could stay on target and see the Desired Result(s) Produced (the DRP) in our careers or businesses?

And what if this were to be followed up by a self-examination, where we asked ourselves: Is my enthusiasm as strong now as when I first started? Am I still abreast of market developments? Do I have written goals? If so, do I consult my goal sheet regularly to see where I am in realizing them? If everyone performed as I do and had my attitude, would the organization and its clients benefit, or would it be a disaster? Would it be a happy place, or one to be avoided? Do I contribute to the corporate good, or feed off it? If I were an employer, would I fire me or hire me? Where do I need to change to be the worker, boss, or leader I want others to be?

I had a salesman who called this a "checkup from the neck up". Captures it pretty well, I think. If you submitted to this kind of corporate and personal maintenance schedule, what would it do for your career, job satisfaction, inner pride, and personal growth? Not to mention the contentment and happiness of others in the workplace.

Now form a mental picture of a corporation where all of the above is part of the culture, and suppose you worked for one where this was not in place. What chance would you and your company have competing with one that had a maintenance schedule and a culture of self-examination?

Make your company one that has a thorough and regular schedule of maintenance. If that's beyond your power, then at least submit yourself to the self-examination described above. This will produce miracles—in your career, and in every other facet of your life too, including marriage and other relationships.

> *"Examine yourselves to see if you are*
> *in the faith; test yourselves."*
> – 2 Corinthians 13:5

> *"For your ways are in full view of the Lord,*
> *and he examines all your paths."*
> – Proverbs 5:21

50

DILIGENCE

The word diligent means "hard-working, industrious, conscien-tious, painstaking," and, according to Rev. Bob Gass, describes a person who's sharp, decisive, trustworthy, and keen. "Does this describe me?" you may be asking yourself. If you're in pursuit of success, be it in the workplace, your studies, your marriage or other relationships, your walk with God, or any other area of life, then I hope you can answer that question with a resounding "Yes!" If, on the other hand, you're not at all sure that these adjectives describe you—or, God forbid, you know they don't—then it's time for some action that will get you on track to realize the success you crave.

What are these actions? How do you become a "diligent" person as described above?

If you've read this far, then be encouraged, as you've already taken the first step to bring about change in yourself: you've had the courage to honestly identify and face a success-breaker in your character, and are looking for answers to help bring about needed change. Total honesty with yourself is the first step on the road to achievement. Once you've identified and squarely faced any deficiencies in your habitual way of thinking and acting, you can then start working on filling in those missing qualities so they become an integral part of who you are.

Now, be careful here: just tackle one at a time, always starting with the easiest bad habit to change. For instance, if up to this point you've been careless about doing as you promised, make up your mind to begin keeping your promises for the next seven days. Share this resolve, with your family and probably with co-workers too, to keep you on target. When you've succeeded, you'll feel the satisfaction of victory, something you may not have felt for a long time.

Then do the same thing for the next seven days, and with another success, a new pride and confidence will begin to set in. Soon you'll be able to tackle the next habit or character trait—for example, resolve to do work of a superior quality or to increase your daily productivity in your workplace.

Set yourself no more than one goal per week at a time. After several weeks of seeing these weekly goals realized, you'll feel that you're actually starting to become a diligent person—and this feeling, in and of itself, this positive sense of who you are, will produce more and more success in many other aspects of your life. You will gradually develop into that hard-working, industrious, decisive, conscientious, and trustworthy person that others can depend on and be proud of! What could be more worthy and honouring than to be known as diligent in your work, relationships, and whatever other tasks come your way? And once you've earned this honour, work to keep it!

> *"What we hope ever to do with ease,*
> *we must learn first to do with diligence."*
> – Samuel Johnson

> *"The plans of the diligent lead to profit as*
> *surely as haste leads to poverty."*
> – Proverbs 21:5

51

YIELDING: THE RELATIONAL LUBRICANT

The "yield" signs—as opposed to stop signs—at merging roads are a great idea, aren't they? They help the flow of traffic without compromising road safety. The trouble begins when drivers refuse to yield, instead barging ahead demanding right of way when it is denied them for good reason at that particular time. The result of refusing to yield often has serious consequences, such as vehicle damage at best, personal injury or even death at worst. Here, yielding at the appropriate time makes sense, doesn't it?

It makes sense when it comes to success in the workplace too, whether you're part of management or an employee. In fact, willingness to yield—with an emphasis on willingness—is an essential part of all wholesome relationships, whether between management and workers or colleagues in a workplace setting, in a marriage or between family members, between neighbours, or in other personal relationships.

Just as the refusal to yield when called for spells trouble for traffic, so does the absence of a willingness to yield in workplace and personal relationships. At work it creates friction and the loss of workplace harmony and happiness, which will eventually adversely affect corporate success and bottom line. In a marriage, unwillingness to yield mostly leads to much heartbreak and distress, often resulting in family breakup and divorce.

Willingness to yield means, first of all, willingness to really listen—openness to the other's point of view, their concerns, objections, and suggestions. It means an attitude of flexibility, not a position set in concrete where it's "my way or the highway". It's an attitude that says, "This is currently my stand, but I'm willing to listen and adjust in response to sound objections or suggestions." To do this properly, you must drop any bias and be prepared to imagine yourself in the position of the other person. When you adopt this attitude, everyone benefits, and the course of action taken will have a good chance of producing the desired result.

Are there moments when yielding is not a wise course? Absolutely! For example, a CFO may need to be unyielding in defending his or her stand when a CEO demands expansion steps in the absence of the necessary funds. On the home front, where children demand parental action that the household budget can ill afford, or that would be morally wrong or too dangerous, parents need to be unyielding. And a Christian needs to be unyielding when asked to perform tasks that would be contrary to Jesus' teaching and thus against their faith and principles.

But a general unwillingness to yield is like an oak tree which—unable to bend with the wind—will be either uprooted or broken. A yielding attitude, on the other hand, is like a willow, able to bend with the wind and to stand in the fiercest storm. Ask God for insight to be wise and discerning about when to yield and when to stand. Author Elizabeth George says, "True wisdom is marked by willingness to listen and a sense of knowing when to yield." And the Bible says:

"Let the wise listen and add to their learning, and let the discerning get guidance."
– Proverbs 1:5

52

WHAT'S IN IT FOR ME?

When presented with a proposal, have you ever said, or found yourself thinking, "What's in it for me?" I know I have. It's a thought we like to keep secret, as it can come across as selfish, and who wants that? Especially if we're Christians, selfishness is the last thing we want to convey. For instance, we wouldn't dare respond with "What's in it for me?"—even though we might be thinking it—when told by God's word that, in the workplace as anywhere else, whatever we are doing we are to "do it all for the glory of God" (1 Corinthians 10:3), or that we should "work with enthusiasm, as though working for the Lord rather than for people" (Ephesians 6:7).

In another passage (Ecclesiastes 9:10), we read, "Whatever your hand finds to do, do it with all your might." All of these texts, translated into everyday language, say that no matter what we are doing, (a) our effort should be wholehearted, and (b) we should do it as an act of worship to the Lord, not just to please our boss—though no doubt he or she would be well pleased also. Yes, if you were to put your whole heart and soul into your work, you'd surely be noticed! But our primary motivation is to delight and glorify God with our work by giving it everything we've got.

Many of us professing Christians fall rather short of this biblical command, don't we? Even though we are, or feel like we are, working our butts off (which is no more than we ought to be doing) it's most often to further our careers or businesses rather than the glory of God. In other words, we're working for personal gain—which makes perfect sense to us. After all, isn't workplace success a legitimate and honourable goal, worthy of God's blessing? But though we want and hope for God's blessing, our thoughts aren't much on trying to please him. Right?

Now let me pose a question: What blessing would we receive if we did exactly what we're told to do in the above Scripture passages? Take a moment to reread them, and then ask yourself, "What's in it for me, if I obey that command?"

Thank you for asking. To answer that question, turn your attention to the familiar story of Joseph. Note that:

1. He'd just suffered a serious setback, as his brothers had turned on him and sold him into slavery;
2. He found himself thrust into a job that he, as a slave, had no choice but to do;
3. There was a choice he did have: to give in to self-pity and resentment and work half-heartedly, or to give the work his best effort as a matter of honour and integrity, to glorify the one true God whom he was representing in that place.

Joseph chose the latter. He was not looking for "success" per se, but his diligent effort and good will reaped God's blessing on his work and on the company he was working for (Potiphar's empire). He also ended up being noticed and promoted until he eventually ran the whole show. That's what we read in Genesis 39: Potiphar gave Joseph complete administrative responsibility over everything he owned. With Joseph there, he didn't worry about a thing—except what kind of food to eat! Talk about being blessed by God—and by his employer.

When we Christians obey God's command regarding how we are to work and for whom, we too will reap God's blessing. We may not follow the same incredible career path that Joseph did. And if we read further, we'll see that Joseph's integrity later landed him in prison due to the wickedness of others. But you can't keep a good man (or woman) down. Ultimately Joseph was restored to a position of honour, where he was able to do a lot of good for a lot of people, and in all of this the reputation of the one true God was upheld.

If at this point there's a "yabbut" (Yeah, but...) in your thinking, get rid of it! The God who blessed Joseph is the same God who'll bless you—at the very least with an inner pride, peace and content-ment, and a sense of proper satisfaction with your accomplishment: all things that the half-hearted worker never tastes. So when it comes to the command to work with all your might to the glory of God, that's what's in it for you. It's a blessing we can't do without, and it is the real meaning of success in the workplace.

"The Lord was with Joseph, so he succeeded in everything he did as he served in the home of his Egyptian master."
– Genesis 39:2

53

THE POWER OF EXPECTATIONS

Positive expectations: Positive results
Negative expectations: Negative results

Yes, that's the right title: I'm talking about the power of expectations for the successful achievement of any worthy goal you are pursuing. This power is extremely important, and often underrated. I've found that a person's expectation level is a great success predictor for any planned action, whether it be the pursuit of a degree, a business, a career or career change, or even a lasting marriage. Given this power, expectations must be examined and tested.

In checking a highly positive expectation level for something I'm planning, I've learned to ask myself whether there's sufficient justification for it. Is it based on realistic assessments and thorough research, or is it only based on excitement, naïveté, and wishful thinking? Some of the failures I experienced in my 65 years in the business world fell into the wishful-thinking category, and could have been avoided had I gone through the exercise of testing my expectations. There's no question that in order to succeed, you must have a very positive expectation level; but it has to be well grounded in reality. I've found that a justified, reality-checked positive expectation has a 90-percent chance of producing a positive result.

Where do negative expectations enter the success and failure picture? If the reality check has changed your positive expectation to a negative one, don't overrule this feeling, as I've done in the past at great expense and wasted effort. If your plan doesn't pass the reality test, drop it! Don't proceed! Or at least, hold off while you do more research, review your plan and make necessary adjustments to it. This may reignite the vision and lead to the success you're hoping for.

Mind you, a negative expectation needs to undergo the same reality check. You may discover that it's based on the fear of failure, which ought never to be the reason for dropping a plan or project. Or perhaps you're overrating the obstacles, or underrating your ability to overcome them. But if a reality check shows the negative expectation to be justified, then don't proceed.

Here are a few all-important questions for you if you're a Christian:

1. When you pray for wisdom, as you should in the planning of any venture or project, do you really expect wisdom to be given, or is it just a hope that may never be realized?
2. What is your expectation of yourself?
3. What do you think God expects of you?

It's not fair to ask you these if I'm not willing to answer them myself. So, here are my answers: When I pray for wisdom, I expect God to give it; I've never been shamed in this expectation. I expect to give my all to any task I accept. And I believe God expects me to strive to XL (excel) at any task he asks me to undertake, including my daily work as an employee or employer.

"In the morning, Lord, you hear my voice; in the morning I lay my requests before you and wait expectantly."

– Psalm 5:3

54

COMMITMENT

When it comes to succeeding in any kind of endeavour, what role does commitment play? I'll use an analogy. If you were to build a fifty-storey office tower or apartment building, what role would your building's foundation play? A vital one, of course! Without a solid foundation, your building would never even make it to the tenth floor, let alone the fiftieth.

It's like that with any goal you want to achieve. Without one hundred percent commitment, you'll find your resolve fading as soon as difficulties and hardships begin to appear. And appear they will! There's just no easy way to achieve any kind of worthy goal, be it a university degree, promotion at work, a lasting marriage, a flourishing business, a successful career, or any other worthwhile thing. Without commitment—the willingness to hang in there, to suffer and even to bleed—you'll soon find yourself on the slippery road to failure. And then you'll start to rationalize your failure, first to yourself and then to others.

I have a saying: Winners have results; losers give reasons. Winners win first of all because they're committed! They've looked at the cost in resources, time, and effort to produce the desired result; and then they've committed themselves to seeing it achieved, in spite of difficulties, setbacks, and obstacles. It's commitment that sees them through to the finish.

Now, let's be careful here: commitment without the needed ability is like a one-winged airplane: it won't fly. But ability without commitment is like a carriage without a horse: it ain't going anywhere either. I think you get the picture. But what does commitment look like?

There's a difference between interest and commitment. When you're interested in doing something, you do it when circumstances permit. When you're committed to something, you accept no excuses, only results. You keep at it until the objective is reached, no matter what. There are only two options regarding commitment: either you're in or you're out. There's no such thing as life in between.

<u>Commitment</u>
- It's what transforms a promise into reality.
- It's the words that speak boldly of your intentions.
- It's the actions which speak louder than words.
- It's making time when there is none.
- It's coming through time after time, year after year.
- It's the stuff character is made of.
- It's the power to change the face of things.
- It's the daily triumph of integrity over skepticism.
- It's daring to make a promise and keep it.
- It's what lasting marriages are built on,
- As well as any goals you may be in pursuit of.

– Rev. Bob Gass

Commitment matters to God, and it should to you.

55

HOW TO FIND YOUR PASSION

Today we hear, or read—those of us who do read—that to be happy and productive in our jobs we have to "find our passion". And if it's not found in the job we have, then we are justified in continually changing jobs in search of it. In fact, such action is encouraged by experts in human happiness.

I'm convinced that this theory creates many unhappy and disgruntled workers. Not having experienced the unleashing of their elusive passion, they keep searching for it elsewhere and don't find it. They go from passionless job to passionless job, where their performance is mediocre at best or unacceptable at worst—and they know it. Such an underperforming and restless worker is generally an unhappy one. And the sad thing is that searching for passion in a different job is largely a fruitless and discouraging search, so the unhappiness continues.

It reminds me of the farmer who sold his farm to search for oil elsewhere, but never found it. After many years of futile drilling, he returned to his old homestead and saw all kinds of oil derricks on the farm he had sold: he had been sitting all along on the oil he went to search for elsewhere. The obvious point is that the passion you are seeking elsewhere can be found and unleashed in the very job you now have!

Passion does not come from outside ourselves; it is already in us, and is released and experienced by workers who, in obedience to God's command, give their all to the jobs God has given them. The command I'm talking about is the one that says, "Whatever your hand finds to do, do it with all your might, as unto the Lord" (Colossians 3:23). No matter what job you're in, this is a command you can passionately follow, just because the Lord is your boss and your work is his gift to you. When you do that, you'll be amazed at how it generates not only more passion, but increased self-respect as well as career opportunities available only to those who are working at their top performance. Just the fact of doing so, out of a wholehearted desire to please the Lord and give quality service to others, creates passion.

Once awakened, this job passion opens up previously unthought-of opportunities. It causes a person to become creative and exercise initiative in looking for ways to excel, causing success that in turn feeds motivation and drive, leading in turn to more passion and more success. Ultimately, just because you are fully exercising your gifts and strengths in what you are doing, your career path will conform to those gifts and strengths.

All of the foregoing is the result of God's blessing on the efforts of his hard-working followers. I have seen this borne out in others, and experienced the truth of it myself when I began to give all I had to the job I held, instead of adding more career changes to the many I had already undergone in the search for my passion.

We see a biblical example of the same thing in Joseph, who, having been sold into slavery, devoted all he had to the job that was not of his choosing, until before he knew it he was promoted to the running of Potiphar's business affairs. Then, when he was falsely accused and found himself in jail, he again pitched in with all he had—and the next thing he knew, he was trusted to run the jail! The ultimate result of this passionate and wholehearted work effort was that he became the Prime Minister of Egypt, and ran the country.

What more evidence do we need? Whatever passion we want to see awakened must be awakened in the job God has given us now, be it as a sweeper, washroom cleaner, factory or office worker, homemaker, farmer, or business owner. Passionately give your all to whatever your hand finds to do, and you'll experience even more passion as well as God's blessing.

> *"Whatever you do, work at it with all your heart, as working for the Lord, not for human masters."*
> – Colossians 3:23

> *"One who is slack in his work is brother to one who destroys."*
> – Proverbs 18:9

56

THE NEED TO ADD

In order to achieve whatever worthy goal we are in pursuit of, and to avoid it slipping out of our grasp once we've achieved it, it's essential to keep adding. Adding what, you ask? Effort, that's what. The unfortunate tendency with many of us is that once we've reached our initial goal, we start coasting, in the mistaken belief that success is now firmly anchored and needs no further attention. But achieved success is like a newly weeded garden that will not remain weed-free without ongoing effort and attention. It must be weeded again and again, and watched carefully so that new weeds can be eradicated as soon as they appear. Or think of a newly filled and treated swimming pool. It requires ongoing attention to stay free of algae and disease-causing bacteria.

It's the same with success in any field, be it business, marriage, career, home, or whatever. And it's like that also in our faith journey: once the initial thrill of a transformed belief system starts to wane, the fledgling Christian needs to keep adding fuel to the fire by way of ongoing Bible study, fellowship with other believers, a vibrant prayer life, and a daily string of choices to act out of love for God and neighbour in all sorts of situations. In all the areas of our lives that matter, there are bad habits we have to keep resisting, and new ones we need to form and maintain—and that takes unceasing attention and effort, like fuel on a burning fire.

So, what's my "keep adding" point? It's a warning to stay alert and not give in to the feeling that "I've worked so hard to get where I am; now I can relax and enjoy the fruits of my hard labour by sitting back and doing little or nothing." Though your success fire may be burning brightly now, you've got to keep adding fuel for it to remain so. The quickest way to see a marriage relationship die is to drop all the input you gave it to bring it to the altar, believing that now the knot is tied, no further effort is needed. As if the marriage can remain a honeymoon for the next 50 years all by itself! Foolish thinking, which leads to destructive behaviour. On the contrary, the brighter the fire, the more fuel it needs to stay bright!

I can think of corporation after corporation, career after career, marriage after marriage, and Christian walk after Christian walk where the attitude that "we've arrived, so now we can sit back and enjoy our success" led to failure—a few dying embers, or a lot of smoke, but no flame. This is sad indeed: had the people involved kept adding fuel to the fire, they would have kept growing and enjoying ongoing success.

Remember: success is a journey, not a destination. So be sure you keep travelling and moving forward. Keep adding to whatever level of success you have thus far achieved.

"So let's not get tired of doing what is good."
– Galatians 6:9

*"That which we persist in doing becomes easier,
not because the task itself has become easier,
but because our ability to perform it has improved."*
– Ralph Waldo Emerson (philosopher, poet, author, essayist)

57

POTENTIAL

Exactly what is potential? I've had a definition of my own for years: potential = not much darn good—yet. Potential is something we all have, to a greater or lesser extent. We might best think of our God-given potential as a gold or diamond mine, or buried treasure, that we may know or suspect is there but is still buried. Until we start digging for it, we'll never know just how much of it there is, or what we can do with it. In other words, it's not much darn good. But there's the "yet": it will be good for something once it's dug up and developed. And yes, I said God-given. God has given each of us the unique gift of our potential. It's different for each of us, and we're the only ones who can make use of it.

We all know that to get at buried gold or diamonds you have to start digging through the soil and blasting through the rocks. It's hard labour, but sure worth the effort when you start bringing all this treasure to the surface, right? Of course, we won't start digging or blasting for this buried treasure unless we believe it's there. Same with our untapped potential: once you overcome your doubts and start believing and accepting that it's there, given by God and living inside you, you'll start digging for it. And then you'll be amazed at what it will do in your home, workplace, career, church, business, and community at large. You'll find yourself experiencing God's blessings and going far, far beyond where you currently find yourself in just about every aspect of your life. It happened for me and it will for you too, but you've got to believe you have potential and then start digging for it and developing it.

Zig Ziglar, a well-known motivational author and speaker, says this about untapped potential: "It's not what you've got, it's what you use that makes a difference."

How to start digging for your potential? Accept that you actually do have untapped God-given potential, and pray for the strength to use it; you'll need strength, because this will involve change. Begin where you are, and go beyond—like the athlete who tries to run a bit faster or farther every day. In the workplace, whether you're a sweeper or the president, go beyond by doing an outstanding job, both in the quality of the work itself and in how you engage with others in your workplace. At home, go beyond by becoming a supportive spouse, parent, or child. At church, become a participant instead of a benchwarmer. And so on.

Once you start, there'll be no stopping you: awakened potential wakes up more potential, in an ongoing upward spiral. I've experienced it and seen it happen in the lives of many. The result of all this unleashed potential will be God's blessing and much happiness for you and your circle of influence, such as your family, colleagues, church family, and community. So, be one to tap in to your God-given potential!

> *"There is no person living who isn't capable of doing more than they think they can."*
> – Henry Ford Sr.

> *"If your gift is to encourage others, be encouraging. If it is giving, give generously. If God has given you leadership ability, take the responsibility seriously. And if you have a gift for showing kindness to others, do it gladly."*
> – Romans 12:8

58

SECOND CHANCE?

If you're an employer or supervisor, what are you to do when one of your star performers is caught in one form or another of dishonesty, such as (at best) a lie, or (at worst) a theft? Yes, it can and does happen. This kind of occurrence may not present a problem to many whose corporate or personal policy is to simply fire the guilty employee. But for a Christian employer or supervisor, that action can be problematic. Aren't we commanded to be forgiving and to give second (and even more) chances? Jesus said to the crowd who had come to accuse and punish the woman caught in adultery, "Let any one of you who is without sin be the first to throw a stone at her" (John 8:7). And then he told the woman he didn't condemn her; she was to go her way unpunished, and stop doing wrong.

So, what do you do? Here's your star performer, a highly valued employee that you're loath to lose, and you find out they've been dishonest.

That's what happened in my case. My secretary received a call from a customer who claimed that my only salesman at the time—we had been in business for just one year—had been cheating him. The customer wanted to see whoever was in charge. Since the buck was supposed to stop with me, I had to go. I had only just started in business, and I had found in this particular salesman—my first—a winner, a uniquely gifted professional. Now I stood to lose him; after all, you can't have a cheater on your staff. What to do?

I met with the rightly upset customer, who told me

what had happened. It was obvious that our salesman had indeed been caught red-handed. I won't relate what it was he did, but will share with you how we handled this very serious situation. I admit that I wasn't motivated solely by charitable and forgiving feelings, but also by a concern about losing this highly gifted salesperson.

I met him on his rounds and relayed the accusation, which he at first denied; but when confronted with the overwhelming evidence—including his having been observed in the act—he turned white and admitted his foolish and wrong action. He was just 21 at the time, and his future was now in shambles—unless. . . !

When I told him that I had no choice but to fire him, he expressed what sounded to me like true regret and asked for a second chance. I appreciated his repentant attitude and told him I would leave it up to the customer, a man in his mid-fifties, whether to fire him or not. We were parked on the customer's business property, so I went in on behalf of my salesman to convey his plea for a second chance.

What saved the culprit was his youth; with the mark of a theft against him at this early age, he'd face a bleak future. This fact is what moved the older man to forgive. When my salesman came in himself to express his remorse and ask forgiveness, our customer—a marvellous human being—talked with him and forgave him. He was offered a second chance, and went on to work for 38 more years in my company.

> *"For if you forgive other people when they sin against you, your heavenly Father will also forgive you."*
> – Matthew 6:14

59

UPHILL

It's true, isn't it, that success is desired by all. However, achieving it in any endeavour, from marriage to a career, university degree, beautiful garden, or clean living accommodation, takes uphill effort. According to John Maxwell (a prominent leadership trainer) the trouble with this struggle is that so many of us have high uphill hopes, but too many destructive downhill habits.

There's another problem as well, and that is the expectation that once you achieve a measure of success in any field, you will be able to relax and take it easy. This is a fallacy that leads straight back downhill. Just think of an airplane: it takes a tremendous amount of energy and power to reach its flying level—and at that point, does the pilot turn the power off? Of course not. No more can you in your success journey, not if you want to continue to enjoy your hard-earned success. Just as a newly-weeded garden has to be weeded again and again in order to stay weed-free, your freshly-achieved success will not remain in place without ongoing effort. It's like that with everything, including your career: just because you've finally attained a corner office on the fiftieth floor, don't think you've reached the time in your life when you can relax and let up on the effort.

Let's take a look at some downhill habits that stand in the way of achievement. Procrastination is one: you need to replace a do-it-tomorrow attitude with a do-it-now attitude if you want to succeed. Poor punctuality, defensive reactions to criticism, and ducking responsibility are also downhill habits, along with sloppiness and a tendency to refuse any task that isn't in your job description. All of these are part of the easy, no-effort way that leads downhill. And you can probably think of other downhill habits.

All success is an uphill climb, a climb that will never end. There is no easy way to achieve it or retain it. Those who want success but do not give it the needed effort are doomed to continue walking in the dust of those who do.

"And may the Lord our God show us his approval and make our efforts successful. Yes, make our efforts successful!"
– Psalm 90:17

"Most worthy endeavours are an uphill battle..."

60

DECISIONS

At my last compulsory senior's driving test (I'm 87), the instructor stated that for every mile we drive we make over a thousand decisions: how close to follow, how fast to drive, whether to ignore or act on the flashing indicator light on the car in the left lane, when to speed up or slow down, whether the car at the exit of the parking lot to our right is about to enter traffic or not, and so on. No wonder transport drivers tire after 500 miles and thousands and thousands of decisions!

Everything we do or don't do is preceded by a decision—even when we think we're not making a decision. Even when we say, "I can't decide," we've just made a decision not to make a decision. That's why we're always held responsible for our actions or inaction, because both are preceded by a decision we made.

What decision have you made regarding your studies, career, business, education, marriage, relationships, income, or savings? What decision have you made about where you want to be in 5, 10, or 30 years? The decisions you make today will determine in no small measure where you will find yourself in the not-too-distant future. Remember that there is no such thing as not making decisions: not making a decision is making one anyway. It simply means you've decided to drift through life and let fate—or "luck", as some call it—decide for you. That's like a sailor leaving the harbour and letting the wind blow him wherever it wants: his likely destination is probably the closest rocky shore and shipwreck.

The unfortunate fact is that there are many whose careers never take off, or whose relationships flounder, not because of a lack of luck but because of a lack of proper decision-making. If I'm right in this, and I am, then those people are personally responsible for the result.

Note that there is always a result, although it may not be the desired one. There's a saying, "Eventually everyone will sit down to a banquet of consequences." Sobering thought, isn't it? The dictionary defines "consequence" as "the result or effect of an action", and we know that an action is the result of a decision. It follows that by our decisions we are able to exercise a lot of control over what happens in our careers, businesses, relationships, education, incomes, savings, marriages, and so forth.

Let's take a look at career. What decision did you make as to the work you would do or what you would become, such as architect, doctor, teacher, electrician, or transport driver? Is the work you are now doing something you just drifted into, or is it the result of a firm decision? If it is not to your liking, what decision will you make to bring about the desired result? You can see, can't you, that it will take a decision to produce a different result?

Decision-making is not only what happens at a few turning points in life, either; it's a daily event. When you went to work today, what kind of effort did you decide to give your job? If you've been having some conflict with a co-worker, what decision have you made regarding corrective action? Are you just going to let things stand as they are? That's a decision. What's your decision about the argument you had with your spouse this morning, or about upgrading yourself by taking some night courses? What's your decision regarding doing some volunteer work, getting more exercise, going to church, or seeking a closer walk with Jesus? In all of the foregoing, your decisions will always have a result, desired or not. Yes, your daily life is filled with decisions—decisions only you can make. And yes, that's why you are held personally responsible for these decisions and their consequences.

What does all of this mean for the Christian who's "waiting" for God's "plan" to unfold for his or her life? Now this may sound rough, but that waiting is no more than a decision not to act—because God's plan for each of us is already clearly laid out in Scripture. When it comes to the workplace, for example, he says, "Whatever your hand finds to do, do it with all of your might," and "Do it as unto the Lord." We are also told what to do with our gifts and abilities. And we are already told how to behave towards others with whom we're in relationship. Each of these directives from God are part of his explicit plan for us, and each one calls for a decision! Are you going to decide to obey or ignore?

God has promised that his plan is good. "'For I know the plans I have for you,' declares the Lord, 'plans to prosper you and not to harm you, plans to give you hope and a future'" (Jeremiah 29:11). But here, too, you have to decide whether God is joking or telling the truth; you have to decide whether to believe or not. If the decision is to believe, then you need to do something God can bless. That means committing to a worthy, thought-out course of action and giving it all you've got. At work, it means doing with all your power whatever your hand finds to do.

As for whether you end up in the "right" career or school or city: if there is such a thing, God will take you there when you're engaged in doing what he has already told you to do. He can only steer a vehicle that is already moving. And obedience in small things leads to bigger opportunities.

In Deuteronomy 28, we read that Moses told the people all the things the Lord would do for them if they obeyed. They were not forced to obey; they were left free to decide Yes or No and were told the consequences in each case. Later on in the story of Israel, Joshua again urged the people to make a decision when he asked them whether they were going to serve the Lord or the gods of the land they were in. He went on to say, "As for me and my house, we will serve the Lord." He had made his decision!

I'll stop here, hoping you get the message: you've received God-given decision-making responsibilities that will affect your future. You can respond by praying, "Lord, please help me make decisions in accord with what you've said in your word." May you be among those who walk in obedience and make decisions worthy of God's blessing.

> *"This he has promised to do if you will only obey him and walk in his ways."*
> – Deuteronomy 28:9

61

GROW

When John Maxwell, a well-known leadership trainer, was asked, "How do you grow an organization?" he responded, "That's very simple: grow yourself."

In other words, according to Maxwell, when you become better, so will your organization. In fact, I think you'll find that as you grow, so does everything and everyone around you: your family, your spouse, your friends, your co-workers. And when one aspect of yourself grows, so does the rest: your ambition, your insight, your daring, and your caring.

So how do you grow? Well, it seems mostly to begin with dissatisfaction with the way things are, which sprouts a desire to see them changed, which in turn leads to the recognition that "if it's to be, it's up to me." If this does not happen, then stagnation, frustration, and likely bitterness will result.

But once this process has taken place in your thinking, you're ready for the next step, which is usually to recognize that change will demand something of you which you don't yet have. This confronts you with a decision: will you, or will you not, commit to cultivating whatever is lacking: a skill, an attitude or disposition, knowledge, a connection with someone—or even a simple willingness to risk. Whatever it is, it is the thing you need to do so that... so that what? The answer to that depends on you.

Notice: the specific, concrete answer to your "so that" is vital to turning your desire into a commitment to grow. An airplane short on fuel will soon run out and crash; so will you, unless you have a specific, concrete "so that"—a statement of purpose or goal. It will be the fuel that keeps you on target and drives you forward when the uphill climb seems endless and the mountaintop seems unreachable. The "so that" is the real reason, the reward, the motivation to stick with the difficult process of growth in whatever area needs development in order to accomplish the desired change. Without it, you're shooting in the dark at an unknown target. Your unfocused efforts will be wasted, your determination will seep away, and you'll give up and decide it can't be done.

Here's an example: "I'll go back to school and upgrade myself so that... I can become a medical doctor." Or a legal secretary. Or a journalist. Or a real estate agent. The clear vision of you as a doctor, or whatever it is, will keep fuelling your determination. Or maybe it's: "I'll take some evening courses so that... I can be considered for a promotion and increase my income for the benefit of my spouse and children." The clear vision of increased earnings and all that will do for your family will fuel your resolve to grow and reach your goal. Or maybe for you it's: "I will take some marriage courses as well as counselling so that... I can see harmony restored in my home and recapture the love we seem to have lost for each other." The vision of living in blessed harmony with a loving spouse will help you hang in there.

Whatever your "so that", as you set out on this path of personal growth, here's something to keep in mind when you fail here and there on your way: it's not failing that makes you a failure; it's quitting, it's refusing to learn from failure, to get back up and continue walking.

"The wise are mightier than the strong, and those with knowledge grow stronger and stronger."
– Proverbs 24:5

62

THE PRAYER OF THE PARTICIPANT

If you're like most of us Christians, then prayer is likely a regular part of your life, especially prayers for things you want or need. These wanting prayers are no doubt much more frequent with most of us than prayers of thanksgiving or worship. But did you know that a vital component is often missing from our wanting prayers, which is the reason that so many of them don't get answered? It took me many years and many unanswered prayers to discover this.

What's the missing part? Well, you know how we'll pray: "Please, Lord, bless my family and let there be harmony." Or about our jobs: "Please, Lord, let me get this promotion," or if unemployed, "Please, Lord, give me a job." All of these are legitimate prayers, but there's a vital component missing: participation. Once these prayers have been sent up, there are two people waiting: you and God. You for God's answer, and God for you to partner with him—to participate in bringing about the outcome you're asking for.

But you may not know what your participation should look like. And you don't want to just go blundering ahead in your own wisdom and energy; we're talking about a partnership: you and God. Your prayer needs to include both your willingness to act and your openness to God's guidance for that action. So what does a "participatory" prayer look like?

Here's the family-harmony prayer with the missing part added: "Please, Lord, bless my family and let there be harmony, and please show me what I have to do to help this become a reality." Here's the unemployed prayer: "Please, Lord, give me a job, and show me what I have to do to bring it about. Show me where to start..." And here's the alcoholic's prayer: "Please, Lord, help me break my drinking habit, and please show me what I have to do to see this realized."

When I started praying this way, God always answered the participatory part of my prayer first, showing me what I had to do; by responding with action, I gave God lots of things he could bless in order to bring about the desired result. My part of the answer to the family-harmony prayer was to be kinder, more patient, and less critical, and when I did this with God's help, harmony was born. When I prayed the job prayer, God said, "Start knocking on door after door after door, and keep doing so until I bless your effort with a job." I did, and he did. God showed me that my part in answering the prayer about my drinking habit was to admit I had a problem, have people pray for me, and join the Celebrate Recovery program. I did, and he set me free!

God knows what we need, but he does no wand-waving; his main project is not changing circumstances, it's changing people. He wants us to partner with him, to become the kind of people who will seek his guidance and strength and then take action with him. That is what he blesses. So start praying in a way that includes your participation; then do what God shows you to see the prayer realized, and see miracles happen.

"O Lord, hear my plea for justice. Listen to my cry for help. Pay attention to my prayer, for it comes from honest lips."
– Psalm 17:1

63

WORK: A BURDEN, OR A DELIGHT?

If I were to ask, "Is your work a burden or a delight to you?" what would be your answer? My hope is that your answer would be "a delight". But unfortunately, according to Forbes, some 40 percent of North Americans are unhappy at their jobs.

For the first five years of my working life I was part of that 40 percent: Monday mornings were most certainly not my favourite. Happily, that changed, and for more than 50 years—out of 60+—I loved my work and looked forward to Monday mornings.

What brought about the change? Was it a different job? No. The change came about when I became a Christian and began obeying God's word: "Whatever your hand finds to do, work at it with all your might and do it as unto the Lord." When I started giving my all—all my might—to my work, it did several things:

- It produced a new sense of inner satisfaction; just knowing that I was doing my best gave me pride and happiness.
- I became a more productive worker.
- I experienced that a job well done has God's blessing: I was noticed, appreciated, and promoted.
- Monday mornings became something to be looked forward to instead of dreaded.

My changed attitude became a habit that stayed with me for most of the 60+ years spent in the labour force, 40 of these in my own business.

What does it take to get to where you can say, "Thank

God for Monday morning too"?

1. Make up your mind that you are done with complaining and half-hearted effort and that from now on you will give your all to whatever work you're currently engaged in.
2. Ask for God's help and blessing on this commitment to changed behaviour. You'll need his help; you can't do it alone.
3. Share your decision with some people whose opinion and advice you value. Not sharing it with someone makes giving up too easy.
4. Expect and accept that the change won't be easy, that the going may get tough. Expecting and accepting this will help you hang in there.
5. Don't delay! Go for it now. A delay mostly becomes "I had good intentions."

"Work willingly at whatever you do, as though you were working for the Lord rather than for people."
– Colossians 3:23

"Work hard and become a leader; be lazy and become a slave."
– Proverbs 12:24

64

BEING STEADFAST

What role does steadfastness play in the success of any endeavour? To give you a full appreciation of its import-ance, let me provide some synonyms for the word "steadfast": unwavering, unswerving, firm, committed, unfaltering... The list could go on.

If you're among the many who haven't achieved the goal they were pursuing, it's quite possible that this many-splendoured quality of steadfastness was lacking in whatever effort you made. The sad truth is that all too often we approach our goal with lots of "hope"—in the sense of "I hope I make it!"—without tying that hope to commitment, determination, stick-to-it-iveness, and a willingness to pay the price. Our hope soon dies when the going gets difficult, when the inevitable problems we never gave a thought to pop up at the most unexpected and unwelcome times and places. And once our hope begins to die, our thinking shifts to "This will never work" or "I just can't do it," which in turn leads to packing it in.

Most people only need to experience a couple of these failures before they retreat forever to their comfort zone, doomed to mediocrity in their careers and every other part of their lives. Success demands that we be steadfast—unswerving, unwavering, committed, unfaltering—which means that we keep putting in a sustained effort right through all the growing pains and problems, dealing with them as they arise and overcoming them. A never-give-up commitment is the first essential step in goal-achieving, whether the goal is related to work or career, marriage or family, ministry, or growth in one's faith life. Ken Poirot, a well-known author, says: "Success awaits those who steadfastly commit to any requisite sacrifice." No one should expect it to be otherwise.

It goes without saying that a Christian puts God first in planning and setting a worthy goal, and looks to God for the strength and wisdom required to deal with obstacles and stay the course. Do this, and you can expect his blessing.

Now go and give your goal that second, third, or even fourth or fifth try—this time with a hopeful attitude and a determination to be steadfast, to press on until the goal has been realized.

That is why we never give up:

> *"Though our bodies are dying, our inner strength in the Lord is growing every day."*
> – 2 Corinthians 4:16

65

FEELINGS, UNCHECKED

Feelings: yes, we all have them, an abundance of them. Unchecked, they can bring a lot of problems to your pursuit of success, whether in your career, marriage, business, studies, walk with Christ, or any other area of life.

Some say that we *are* our feelings. But this is a dangerous and limiting way to think. If your feelings define you, if they're the governing force in your behaviour, you have no option but to follow their lead. You may well end up doing something that torpedoes your chances of success, or doing nothing when success requires action.

Not following me? Perhaps an example will help. Say you've just signed up for a university course, feeling great about your decision to upgrade yourself and having every intention of giving it your all and finishing the course. But once you get started, your feelings change. You find you just don't feel like studying or working on assignments this particular night, and you have a similar feeling the next night. And then the night or day after that you just don't feel like attending classes. And so it goes. If you let your feelings determine your actions because they are you, what do you think will happen as far as completing your course?

Especially in our teen years, feelings are often unchecked and lead to quitting school because they are allowed to control actions. Later, the same thing happens with work: a person doesn't feel like getting up in the morning, or doing work that seems hard or dull or complicated. Giving in to these feelings results in losing job after job. I know, because that's what happened to me.

Some people never outgrow this tendency to let unchecked feelings control their behaviour, and consequently they continue to reap failure in so many areas of life. Thankfully, I learned not to give my feelings this kind of power, and then I was able to soar—in the workplace, in my marriage and family life, in my faith, and in my walk with Christ.

So how does one handle these feelings? *I don't feel like it. I feel afraid. I feel hurt. I feel used. I feel angry. I feel like quitting. I feel I'm in over my head. I feel like giving up.* Here's what I do: I acknowledge these feelings and don't try to deny them. Then I answer them: "Thank you, Feelings, for sharing your status with me, and now let me respond to you: I'm not quitting, I'm not giving up, and I'm going to be able to deal with the hurt or disappointment. I'll handle the difficulties. AND now, you be quiet, as you're a distraction." And you know what? The feeling-voice shuts up and lets me go back to achieving.

So, instead of allowing your unchecked feelings to ride roughshod over your intentions and goals, have the discipline to accept your feelings without letting them control you. It's not easy, though! And it takes fresh resolve every day. So if I were you, I'd ask God to help me, every day.

66

THERE'S A PRICE TO PAY IF...

Yes: there's a price to pay if you refuse to accept and adjust to change. Change is inevitable. Period. It's futile to try to prevent it or pretend it's not happening. So if you're in pursuit of success and achievement in any field or endeavour, and over time you refuse to accept change and adjust to new circumstances, you'll very likely find yourself paying the price: failure. Let me give you a today example that clearly illustrates what I'm talking about.

Consider that segment of the First Nations people who've refused to accept the changes that have come upon all nations and peoples over the last several hundred years. Many of the First Nations people are struggling to sustain or revive a past that—for better or for worse—is gone forever. Since today's world will no longer support their former pre-technological lifestyle of living on the land, hunting, fishing, and trapping, the First Nations' effort to hang on to that lifestyle is worse than useless, because it only serves to marginalize them further. The result is maladjustment that leads to all kinds of problems. The only way they can manage to limp along in their state of denial without facing total demise is by continuing to receive money from the government.

(CAVEAT: I don't mean to ignore the role played by the oppression and violence perpetrated against the First Nations by earlier generations of Europeans—for which the current system of reserves and handouts is a sort of penance. But if it is a penance, it's also a backhanded way of inviting the First Nations to remain stuck in their time warp. It is easier for them to accept "help" that erodes their dignity and initiative, discourages achievement, and prevents responsible leadership from developing among them, than to take the first difficult steps to embrace change and deal with it. Unable to pursue their traditional lifestyle, and unprepared to succeed in the one that has replaced it, their communities suffer a lack of purpose and focus, leading to the anguish of family breakup, addiction, suicide, prostitution, and violent crime.)

But if their situation is complicated, there are nevertheless some who have grabbed the bull by the horns, made a supreme effort of imagination, figured out how to maintain their identity while adapting to a new reality even at this late stage in the game, and taken action. And they have succeeded, some of them turning to help others in their community do the same.

Meanwhile, your situation is likely not so complicated. Quite simply: there's a price to pay if you refuse to accept and adjust to change, and the price only gets higher the longer you try to hold out. You may not like the change you face; you may even hate it. But you'd better accept it and learn to adapt, because like it or not, change will come and you can no more hold it back than you can hold back a tsunami. Those who refuse to accept and adjust to change will find themselves left behind, frustrated, likely resentful, and facing a dismal future filled with failure, disappointment, and disaster. To live a successful life of achievement and happiness in the workplace, and in every other area of life, you have to accept change and adjust accordingly.

*"To enjoy your work and accept your lot in life—
this is indeed a gift from God."*
– Ecclesiastes 5:19

67

TALENT

Leo Buscaglia, a well-known university professor, said, "Your talent is God's gift to you. What you do with it is your gift back to God." To which I will add, "and, secondly, a gift to yourself—that is, if you use your talents in an honourable way."

In my 86 years of life on this planet—66 of them in the workplace—I've met a lot of people who believe they have no special talents and conclude that this is the reason they don't experience success. In other words, fate has dealt them a talentless hand, so what's the use in trying? Should you find yourself in that I-have-no-talent mindset, here's something that will help you uncover your God-given talent, find new hopes of success, and achieve it.

Talent is only discovered and set free in us when we are striving to excel in whatever task is at hand. Whether in the workplace, relationships, marriage, or any other sphere of life, talent lies dormant in the presence of mediocre effort. When I entered the workplace, I was in the habit of making just such a mediocre effort, and was soon filled with resentment and envy of all those talented and gifted folks whose success-dust I was eating. This in turn caused me to drift from mediocre to outright useless.

My wake-up call came when I found myself finally out of money, out of friends to borrow from, desperate, jobless, and with holes in my shoes. It dawned on me that it was not my lack of talent but my lack of genuine effort that had brought me to this sad state of affairs. I began to realize that I was reaping what I had sown, and that if I changed my level of input there would be a different result. The problem was not fate or lack of talent; it was me!

With new knowledge and new resolve—acquired the hard way—I gave my all to the job I eventually managed to secure. This new attitude and new all-out effort led in time to promotion after promotion, and ultimately to my own successful business. As I moved forward and upward in responsibility, I noticed a talent for leadership emerging, and other people noticed it too; and as I continued to give a whole-hearted effort to my work, I found (and was given) opportunities to use my talent and to further hone and develop it.

But my leadership talent was only found, released, and developed as a result of all-out effort. God gives all of us talents, but they remain undiscovered if there is no challenge causing them to emerge. Only an all-out effort provides the context for a talent to become noticeable. And such an effort must start with the small things, jobs that may be seen and felt as unimportant (though there really is no such thing), before there can be any advance towards greater, more challenging, and more rewarding responsibilities.

Discovery of one's talent is the reward for pushing oneself to do one's best. Would you give more resources or responsibility to someone who does little with the opportunities already entrusted to them? Of course not! Neither does God. As the saying goes: "If you don't make a good sweeper, you'll not make a good president."

"So, to find and unlock your God-given talent(s), give your absolute ALL to whatever your hand finds to do!"

– Joe Schuringa

ACKNOWLEDGMENTS

Thanks are due to editor Debbie Sawczak, whose finely tuned ear added polish to the manuscript; and to my LifeWork Project team – Jeremy King, Jim Poopalapillai and Daniel Ramlogan – for their shared passion and creative vision.

ABOUT THE AUTHOR

Johan F. Schuringa is a retired businessman. Beginning from almost nothing, he built up a thriving enterprise through hard work and God's blessing. Since retiring, he has helped lead Celebrate Recovery and served on the boards of several charities and institutions. Today, he lives in Georgetown, Ontario, and heads up the LifeWork project (www.lifeworkproject.org). He is also the author of *The Cows Must Be Milked* and the forthcoming LifeWorkBook. And he is an avid grandfather.